CAMBRIDGE LIBRARY COLLECTION

Books of enduring scholarly value

British and Irish History, Nineteenth Century

This series comprises contemporary or near-contemporary accounts of the political, economic and social history of the British Isles during the nineteenth century. It includes material on international diplomacy and trade, labour relations and the women's movement, developments in education and social welfare, religious emancipation, the justice system, and special events including the Great Exhibition of 1851.

Perran-Zabuloe

The curate William Haslam (1817–1905) focuses here on the ruins of St Piran's oratory, for many years lost to Cornwall's shifting sands. First published in 1844, his work laments the site's fate: first destroyed by its environment, then, upon its rediscovery, pillaged by trophy hunters. Highlighting the importance of Cornwall's frequently overlooked ecclesiastical antiquities, of which the oratory is perhaps the most compelling example, Haslam also gives an account of his local parish. The work describes the surrounding landscape, before going into an analysis of the oratory itself, with a small number of accompanying illustrations. An account of the life of St Piran, who has come to be regarded as Cornwall's patron saint, complements the history of Christianity's growth in the area, which resulted in the oratory's construction. With a strong emphasis on the oratory's importance as an early Christian site, this study will appeal to readers interested in architectural, church and local history.

T0370854

Cambridge University Press has long been a pioneer in the reissuing of out-of-print titles from its own backlist, producing digital reprints of books that are still sought after by scholars and students but could not be reprinted economically using traditional technology. The Cambridge Library Collection extends this activity to a wider range of books which are still of importance to researchers and professionals, either for the source material they contain, or as landmarks in the history of their academic discipline.

Drawing from the world-renowned collections in the Cambridge University Library and other partner libraries, and guided by the advice of experts in each subject area, Cambridge University Press is using state-of-the-art scanning machines in its own Printing House to capture the content of each book selected for inclusion. The files are processed to give a consistently clear, crisp image, and the books finished to the high quality standard for which the Press is recognised around the world. The latest print-on-demand technology ensures that the books will remain available indefinitely, and that orders for single or multiple copies can quickly be supplied.

The Cambridge Library Collection brings back to life books of enduring scholarly value (including out-of-copyright works originally issued by other publishers) across a wide range of disciplines in the humanities and social sciences and in science and technology.

Perran-Zabuloe

*With an Account of the Past and Present State
of the Oratory of St Piran in the Sands*

WILLIAM HASLAM

CAMBRIDGE
UNIVERSITY PRESS

CAMBRIDGE
UNIVERSITY PRESS

University Printing House, Cambridge, CB2 8BS, United Kingdom

Published in the United States of America by Cambridge University Press, New York

Cambridge University Press is part of the University of Cambridge.
It furthers the University's mission by disseminating knowledge in the pursuit of
education, learning and research at the highest international levels of excellence.

www.cambridge.org
Information on this title: www.cambridge.org/9781108067850

© in this compilation Cambridge University Press 2014

This edition first published 1844
This digitally printed version 2014

ISBN 978-1-108-06785-0 Paperback

RUINS OF THE ORATORY OF S^T PIRAN, IN THE SANDS

London: John Van Voorst, Paternoster Row.

PERRAN-ZABULOE;

WITH AN ACCOUNT OF

THE PAST AND PRESENT STATE

OF

THE ORATORY OF ST. PIRAN IN THE SANDS,

AND

𝕽emarks on its 𝕬ntiquity.

BY THE REV. WM. HASLAM, B.A.

RESIDENT CURATE.

LONDON:

JOHN VAN VOORST, PATERNOSTER ROW.

M.DCCC.XLIV.

LONDON:

Printed by S. & J. BENTLEY, WILSON, and FLEY,

Bangor House, Shoe Lane.

PREFACE.

THE substance of this little work was read in a paper at an evening meeting of the Cornwall Royal Institution; and at the request of the Members of that Institution, and others assembled upon the occasion, is now published, and to them respectfully dedicated, with very many apologies for the unavoidable delay which has taken place in bringing it forward.

It has been deemed necessary to add to the original matter of the paper, a brief introduction to the ecclesiastical antiquities of Cornwall; in order to suit this book for general publication, and a few other matters connected with the early history of this parish have been inserted, which we trust will not be unacceptable.

Cornwall abounds in antiquities, and among these a large and interesting portion are Church antiquities, which seem to be little known. It is true, Cornwall is but a small part of England,

and situated in a remote corner ; its early ecclesiastical and architectural antiquities seem to
have been overlooked in the national theories on
the subject ; but, nevertheless, they have peculiarity enough, and character enough, to stand
as exceptions, or at any rate to be entirely free
from theories which are formed upon other data,
distinct from and different to themselves. We
have antiquities here, and monuments of the
original inhabitants of this island previous to
the Saxon invasion, which need but to be known
and they will be valued. They are in reality
the antiquities of a people who lived in earliest
times, not only in Cornwall but in all Britain;
and therefore may be regarded as a remnant of a
large class which once prevailed throughout the
land. Hitherto writers seem quietly to have
followed one another in attributing civilization
and arts, and even the establishment of the Church
in this island, to the Saxons ; but it is unnecessary now to maintain such opinion. Civilization
and the arts, we have great reason to believe, came
first to the Saxons from the ancient *Irish*, from
whom the few unconquered Britons that remained received the same ; and, as to the esta-

blishment of the Church, no one now is so bold as
to deny that it was planted here long before the
time of St. Augustine. Here is the mistake ; the
Saxons, unnationally, have been made to supersede
the original inhabitants of the island. Their history has been regarded as that of all Britain ;
their antiquities have been made the boast and
pride of antiquaries, and the data of national
theories on architecture and Church history. All
this might have been permitted and submitted as their right, had the Saxons conquered
all Britain : but there are certain portions of the
said Britain they did not conquer for centuries ;
in these parts we should look for our earliest
properly *national* antiquities, and by all means
place them above those of the invaders of the
land. We would not revive a feud and jealousy
which have long, long since subsided ; nevertheless, in treating of the antiquities of these times,
it is impossible to overlook the feelings which
prevailed so strongly, especially as they have set
a mark of distinction, as it were, upon the respective antiquities of these hostile, people. Our
task has been to endeavour to restore to the
oratory of St. Piran some centuries of hoary

antiquity, which have been, we imagine, taken from it by writers who have pronounced it Norman : that it is not Norman there cannot be a doubt, and we are convinced no one who sees the ruin will continue to maintain that it is so ; that it may not be attributed to the Saxons of old, so hostile to Britain, will also appear equally clear when we enter upon their history. We presume then that the oratory of St. Piran is British, or at any rate not Norman.

The term " oratory " has been used, not in the modern acceptation of it, but in that which was received at the period to which we refer the date of this structure, and as the term adopted by subsequent though still early writers with reference to this period. "Oratory" signifies a house of prayer ; not necessarily a private chapel, but a church, the house of God, which is especially a " house of prayer."

W. H.

Lambriggan, St. Perran-zabuloe,
August 30th, 1844.

PERRAN-ZABULOE.

INTRODUCTION.

THE discovery and " restoration" of the ancient
Church of St. Piran, which had for centuries been
lost in the sand, has been already announced in a
work of much interest and popularity by the Rev.
Collins Trelawney. In this work, the church is
considered to have been built in the sixth century,
and to be, without doubt, an early specimen of the
stone building of the British Christians. This is
an opinion which an examination of this interesting structure cannot fail to suggest ; and an opinion, moreover, which is fully borne out by the
strongest probabilities. But it would appear, the
Reverend author has not dwelt sufficiently on the
proofs of his just assertions of its early date ; for,
notwithstanding the strong claims which this
church most certainly possesses to very high
antiquity, doubts seem to be entertained respecting it. They are doubts, however, which might

B

have passed unnoticed but for the authority on
which they partly rest. Mr. Bloxam, in his "Prin-
ciples of Ecclesiastical Architecture," pronounces
"this ruinous structure, which some suppose to
have been an ancient British church," to be "probably not of earlier date than the twelfth century."
It may appear presumptuous to oppose the de-
cision of one, who is justly and deservedly of
high authority in matters of English ecclesiastical
architecture : but, with all deference, I would
submit another opinion, and do so with the more
confidence, as I have had opportunities and faci-
lities of examining this particular subject, which,
I believe, Mr. Bloxam has not had ; and besides I
have reason to believe that Mr. Bloxam has never
seen this church, and that he has had but imperfect accounts, and even worse illustrations,
whereon to found his opinion.

But, with respect to doubts and objections which
are entertained as to the antiquity of this church,
the question may justly be asked, Upon what
ground can such doubts fairly rest ? By what
standard are we to judge the date of a British
structure ? and by what authority may we pronounce, in opposition to every probability and every
evidence, that the structure is not British ? The
histories and theories of the rise and progress of
architecture, which are in general use, and upon
which general opinions and decisions on the subject are formed, are, it must be remembered,

histories and theories of Saxon architecture, *not* British; they are derived from Saxon sources, and confirmed by Saxon authorities. These, surely, cannot be justly applied to British remains. The early ecclesiastical remains of Cornwall (as also of Wales and Ireland) are of earlier date than Saxon, and besides are peculiar in their character; they cannot therefore by any means be made subject to Saxon rules of architecture.

A short insight into the history of the British Church, especially the branch of it in Cornwall, will shew us how great is the distinction between British and Saxon. They were not only a distinct people, but a people hostile to each other, between whom little, and no amicable, intercourse was maintained; and, more than these, they were members of distinct and separate branches of the Church Catholic, upholding with jealous tenacity their own respective rites and customs. This last, it will be seen, is by no means an unimportant distinction, but one which has, as it were, set its mark upon the respective antiquities of these hostile people.

The Church in Cornwall, and, I think we may venture to add, the Church throughout ancient Britain, when organised and established after the Diocletian persecution, was a branch of the Eastern Church, or rather, we should say, of the Church in Asia; for as yet the distinctions of Eastern and Western, Greek and Latin, had not arisen. We readily admit, that St. Paul or his companions from Rome (afterwards the seat of the Western Church) planted Christianity in this island ; indeed we are all bound, in deference to the high authority upon which it is asserted, to admit this : but we venture, upon the evidence of records and antiquities, to add, that the Church planted by St. Paul was nurtured and cultivated, if not replanted, by missionaries from the East; for the Church in the time of the Romans, and after their departure in the time of the British, continued in the observance of rites and cere- monies, which, when the schism between the East- ern and Western Churches took place, proved to be those of the former. Nor will this appear at all improbable when we remember the intercourse and communication the Romans had opened be- tween Byzantium and Britain.

An interesting monument, among others, of the Eastern origin or the Eastern nurture of the early British Church may be traced in our word "*Church;*"* derived from Κυριακὸν, " the Lord's house." This is a word which is often used in the eastern councils of Ancyra and Laodicæa. It

---

* Beveridge, Not. in can. xv. Con. Anc.—" Quum autem hæc (Κυριακὸν) communis fuerit majoribus nostris ecclesiæ cujuslibet templive denominatio, veri nobis simillimum vide- tur, prima Christianæ religionis semina a Græcis huc dispersa fuisse. Neque enim existimandum est, quod Latini Græcum nomen ecclesiis imponerent."

is used by Eusebius, who was a member of the Eastern Church, and is the very name by which Constantine called his churches. The Church thus planted in these isles continued for some time, struggling against the superstition and cruel obstinacy of the people,—"blessing though persecuted," till the conversion of Constantine the Great, early in the fourth century. After this it was openly tolerated, and became the acknowledged religion of the land; but it was not long permitted to enjoy this protection and rest. About the year 420, the Romans, pressed by enemies at home, were compelled to leave Britain, where they had sojourned for four hundred years.

No sooner had they withdrawn their protection than the Picts and Scots invaded the almost defenceless Britons, who in their distress, having urgently appealed for help to Rome in vain, were at length induced to seek the assistance of the Saxons. These accordingly came, and afforded the implored succour; but, perceiving the enervated state of the Britons, turned upon them. Conscious of their own strength, the Saxons proceeded to take possession of the lands they had been invited to defend, and, in order to effect their purpose, had recourse to acts of violence more cruel almost than those of the former invaders. They not only seized the possessions of the Britons, but persecuted them for their religion;

slew their bishops and priests at the very altars,
and demolished their churches,—those which they
had assisted the Romans in erecting, as well as
those consecrated from other uses.*

Thus persecuted and ejected from the fertile
and central parts of their country, the Britons
fled to the mountains of Wales and Cornwall,
where they maintained their independence and
hostile feeling against the Saxons for centuries
after. Here in security they continued, for a
time, in spite of their enemies to observe the
peculiar customs of their Church ; and it is a
remarkable circumstance, in support of the theory
we submit, that the remnant of the British Christians who fled from Saxon persecution to the
mountains and fastnesses of their country, are
found in those places, following the rites of the

* " Hujus persecutionis in anno ccccLXII. Historia ita memi-
nit. Ecclesias et ecclesiastica omnia ad solum usque destrue-
bant, sacerdotes juxta sua altaria trucidabant, sacras scripturas
igne concremabant, per sanctorum martyrum sepulturas cumu-
los terræ congerebant. Eadem repetit Johannes Fordanus in
Scotichronico. Viri religiosi et conjugati substantiam, con-
juges liberos, et (quod majus est) libertatem relinquentes ex-
teras et transmarinas petebant regiones. Nonnulli de mise-
randis reliquiis, qui ab hac clade evadere poterant, speluncas
et nemoralia loca, quidamque boreales partes et quidam aus-
trales, Scotiam videlicet, Walliam, et Cornubiam petierunt, quos
Gildas, qui a calamitissima illa tempestate proxime abfuit, ita
deplorat. Nonnulli miserarum reliquiarum a montibus depre-
hensi acervatim jugulabantur."—Ussher, Britt. Eccl. Antiqu.
c. xii.

Eastern Church, when the earliest light of history falls upon them. Venerable Bede, writing of the "Britons" of his time, speaks of them as confirmed in these customs. In Cornwall, the contests for superiority between the British and the Saxons lasted nearly five hundred years, and were conducted on the part of the former with fortitude and perseverance, notwithstanding the disproportion in numerical force. On the other hand, the Saxons also persevered; in their Heathen and Christian state they were equally hostile. After their conversion, early in the seventh century, by St. Augustine, a missionary of the Western or Latin Church, they seem to have returned to the unequal contention with even increased animosity; not content with invading the secular rights of the Britons, they came now to force the customs of the Western Church upon them. Soon after his settlement in Canterbury, St. Augustine invited the British bishops, seven in number, to meet him in conference. The place of meeting appointed was beneath a large oak-tree (the spot where it stood is still shewn) in Bristol. Here he pleaded with them for subjection to the Bishop of Rome, and for conformity to the Western rites in the observance of Easter, and other matters. But the British bishops answered positively, and in a spirit which seems to have characterised the intercourse between the British and Saxons to the last, that

they owed no obedience to the Pope of Rome.
A copy of their protest* is still preserved by
Sir H. Spelman in his Concilia. The British were so far, says Bingham, from
paying deference to the Romish customs that they
continued their practice of observing Easter on a

---

* " A Protestacōn of the Bīpps in Briten to Augustine the
Monke, the Pope's Legate, in the yeare 600 p't D'm Chrūm.

" Bid ispis a diogel i, chwi ynbod ni holl, vn ac arral, yn vuidd
ac ynn ostingedig i eglwys Duw, ac ir paab o Ruvam, ac i boob
kyar grisdic n dwyucl, y garu pawb yn i radd mewn kariad
parfaich, ac ihelpio pawb o honaunt ar air a guecthred i vod
yun blant y Duw, ac amgenach wyddod ne hwn nidadwen i
vod ir neb yr yddeck chwi y henwi yn paab ne in daad o
daad, yn glemis ac yw ovunn : ar uvyddod hi vn iddem in yw
varod yw rodde ac yw dalu iddo ef ac i pob krisdion yn drag-
widdol.   He wid yr ydym ni dan lywodrath esoob Kaerllion
or Wysc, yr hien ysidd yn oligwr dan Duw ar nom ni, y
wuenthud i ni gadwr fordd ysbrȳdol."—Sir H. Spelman, from
an Ancient British MS. of Peter Mostyn, Welsh gent.   Spelman, Concilia.

" Be it known, and without doubt, to you, that we all are,
and every one of us, obedient subjects to the Church of God,
and to the Pope of Rome, and to every godly Christian, to
love every one in his degree in perfect charity, and to help
every one of them by word and by deed to be the children of
God.   And other obedience than this I do not know due to
him whom you name to be Pope, nor to be the Father of
Fathers, to be claimed and to be demanded.   And this obedience we are ready to give and to pay to him and to every
Christian continually.   Besides, we are under the government
of the Bishop of Caerleon-upon-Uske, who is to oversee under
God to us, to cause us to keep the way spiritual."—Fuller,
Book II. cent. vii. sec. 3.

different Sunday, notwithstanding all the arguments that the Pope and his party could urge against them, for which reason they were treated as schismatics and excommunicated.

"Excommunicated" they remained,—hard and obstinate, inflexibly fond of liberty, and implacable against all conquerors. They knew not how to acknowledge themselves subdued ; and, after a defeat, only waited till the victor had disappeared in order to reinstate their affairs. "The Britaines," says Camden, "in Cornwale so fenced thee countrey and defended themselves that to the raigne of Kinge Athelstan they held out against the Saxons, who, sub*dueing* the western partes, made Tamar* *the bounder* betwixt them and his English, whose last erle of British bloud was Candarus."

In a few years Athelstan extended his conquest into Cornwall, and at length drove the Cornish to the Land's End. Here they made their final stand for liberty, and were overthrown in a terrible battle, the theatre of which is still preserved in the name "Bolloit," a place of slaughter.

Here then, and not till the year 936, did the civil and religious contention between these people cease. For the space of five hundred years the

* In the reign of King Egbert, in 800, who was the first King of all Saxons, as Athelstan afterwards was of all England, the river Ex was the "bounder betwixt them," and half the city of Exeter belonged to the British.

Cornish Britons defied the Saxons, and retained their liberty and the peculiar *rites* of their Church. To the strong and marked character of this period must we advert, in order to estimate rightly the antiquities of the early British Church.

The only traces which remain in Cornwall to the present time of the Saxons are certain customs of the Latin Church, substituted in the place of the Eastern observance, and Saxon names. Though we have records of several churches built and rebuilt by them, no vestiges of Saxon architecture have yet been found here. Names, and the establishment of the rites of the Western Church above alluded to, alone are the monuments of the Saxon conquest. They changed the Roman name Cornubia, which had been derived from the British or Celtic *kernou*, "a horn," (from the shape of the promontory,) into Corn-wealas, to distinguish the land of Cornish Britons from that of the Welsh, which they had already conquered and denominated Wealas. They also altered the division of hundreds in Cornwall, and substituted the present names instead of their ancient ones. They seem to have conquered Cornwall merely for the sake of conquest, in order to indulge hostile feelings, and the bitter animosity which they entertained towards the British ; a circumstance we should never forget, if we would judge fairly between the respective antiquities of these people.

We have seen then that there never existed any
social intercourse between the British and Saxons.
The silence of Venerable Bede with respect to
the British who were contemporaneous with him,
fully confirms this position, and proves that histories and theories of architecture, which have
originated with them, cannot be applicable to
Cornwall at least.

Now, the chief objection to the alleged antiquity of St. Piran's Church seems to rest on a
supposition that churches were built of wood and
wattles daubed with mud, and not of stone, at
this early period. There is Venerable Bede's
authority for the supposition. He says, there was
a time when there was not a stone church in all
the land, but the custom was to build them of
wood. He gives examples, too, of this manner
of building. Paulinus built an oratory of wood,
in which to baptize Edwyn King of Northumbria,
in 627. Finan built a cathedral in Lindisfarne
of wood, and several others ; but these, it must
be remembered, are Saxon examples of a Saxon
theory. They cannot be any guide to British
customs. But he proceeds to add an important
exception to his rule. He records that St. Ninian
built a church of stone so early as 448, in Scotland ; and, in accordance with the impression on
his mind, adds, " insolito more Britonibus."—Bed.
iii. 4. Other historians, however, seem to think
differently of British structures. William of

Malmesbury, fol. 155, records of St. Ninian's
Church, " ecclesiam ibi lapide polito Britonibus
miraculum fecerit ;" thus placing the singularity
of this edifice, not as Venerable Bede, in the circumstance that it was built of stone, but in that
it was built of stone in a *peculiar manner.* Archbishop Ussher, quoting Matthew of Paris, takes
the same view of the case: he says, " ecclesiam *de
albis lapidibus* Britonibus insolitam," etc. These
writers evidently imply that the British built
their churches with stone so early as the fifth
century, and seem to endeavour to qualify the
passage in the history of Venerable Bede on the
subject. Not that the British did not build of
wood, or the Saxons of stone ; but it is contended
the former built not exclusively of wood. Besides
the testimony adduced, we have evidence that
three churches were built in Cornwall, and one
at least was of stone, so early as the year 412.
The British Christians, under St. Patrick's directions, erected a church of stone in a place which
has ever since been known by the name of Patrick or Petroc-stowe* (contracted into Padstow),

* The name " Petroc-stow," or " Padstow," is not the original name of this place, for " stow" is Saxon. It is not unlikely that originally it was called " Patrick :" there is a small
parish bordering on it called " Little Petheric" to this day.
After the conquest of Cornwall, Athelstan named this place
" *Athelstowe*," a presumptuous Saxon alteration ! equalled only
by the audacity of the Roman emperor who desired his statue

at which place the same holy man founded a
monastery, the earliest on record in England.
And, again, there are several amphitheatres and
hill-castles in the west of Cornwall built of stone.
One of the former (now almost utterly destroyed)
stood in the Church-town of St. Just, in Penwith.
These surely are enough to prove that the early
Cornish were not entirely ignorant of the art of
building with stone.

But why is it improbable that the British knew
the art of building with stone. Tacitus informs
us that the Romans, by their assistance, built
temples at a very early period. He also describes the manner in which they imbedded
stones in the mortar, a peculiarity which we
shall have occasion to notice hereafter. Why,
then, it may be asked, may not the British
have retained this simple art, though they certainly had not the skill of the Roman mason, and
seem to have lost the knowledge of the use of
lime, or rather, perhaps, the manner of preparing
it for use. Even supposing the improbable case,
that the Romans took away the art with them,
and that consequently the British lost it, their
intimate communion with the Irish, who knew

to be erected in the Temple at Jerusalem! This name, however, continued till after the time of Leland, and was then
again changed, by uniting the beginning of the former and the
end of the latter together, and thus was formed the Irish-
British-Saxon name *Padstow.*

the art, must have restored it to them very soon
after the departure of the Romans.

Thus far we have shewn that the Cornish were
a distinct people and hostile to the Saxons, and
that no amicable intercourse existed between
them ; let us now consider briefly the peculiar
character of the Church in Cornwall. This subject will bring us at once upon the intimate communion which existed between the Irish and the
Cornish. At the remote period of which we have
been treating, even after Christianity was openly
tolerated and established under the Romans,
Druidism still in a measure continued to prevail
throughout Britain, especially in Cornwall. Such
was also the case in Ireland till the end of the
fourth century, when St. Patrick went forth with
his high commission, to dispel the gloom of the
horrible religion under which his countrymen were
perishing, within sound of the glad tidings of
the Gospel. The success with which his labours
were blessed has handed down his name to posterity as the Apostle and patron saint of Ireland. To
him the Cornish also are indebted for having been
instrumental in furthering the same pious object
here, in Cornwall. He not only laboured among
them in person, to convert them from the errors
of Druidism, but he founded three monasteries
here ; and, on his return to his own country, he
consecrated twelve bishops, most of whom he sent
hither to carry on the great work which he had

been permitted to begin. The most famous of these were St. Petroc, who succeeded him in Padstow, and remained there till his death, and was buried there; * St. Piran, who became the patron saint of Tinners in Cornwall, of whom hereafter; and St. Columb, whose fame is not confined to Cornwall alone. By this means was the Church in Cornwall, not planted, for it had long been introduced, under the Romans, but being established and strengthened, when the Britons from other parts retreated hither for safety from the Saxons. So rapidly did the good work proceed, that in the beginning of the seventh century, when St. Augustine held conference with the British bishops, the Church had been fully established, and was then in strict observance of the rites and discipline of the Eastern Church, and evidently determined to remain so, as we have seen from their protest. Were it not for the probability that the Eastern customs we have referred to, were introduced through Byzantium in the time of the Romans, and for the very early remains which are found in Britain possessing certain marks which, at the great controversy, proved to be those of the Eastern Church, we

* St. Petroc's shrine was plundered by the Danes in 950; and after this his remains were removed to Bodmin. It may be remarked here, that the Danes sided with the Cornish against the Saxons, and did not plunder any part of Cornwall till after it had been conquered.

should be induced to suppose that these customs were brought over by the Irish missionaries, who flocked into Cornwall, especially between the fifth and the eighth centuries. There is no doubt, however, that, if they introduced them not, they at least strengthened and confirmed the British in the observance of them. That the Church in Ireland from the earliest times had received and observed these customs is evident from the following record of a Council which was held at Whitby in Yorkshire, in order to come to some agreement respecting the time of celebrating Easter, in the year 664. St. Colman, an Irishman and Archbishop of York,* entered into dispute with Wilfred, a Saxon priest, on the subject. St. Colman defended the Irish method of calculating the day for holding Easter, saying, " that it had

* It may appear strange that an Irishman, and a member of the Eastern Church, should hold so important an office in the Saxon Church ; but the difficulty will be partly removed by the following extracts. Venerable Bede says of the Irish, that as "a nation they were most friendly to the *English*," and that they were instrumental in converting many of the Saxons and their kings to Christianity. From others we learn that the Irish were the instructors and tutors of the Saxons, and that the latter obtained from the Irish the use of letters ; " for," adds Camden, " they plainly used the characters which are in use among the Irish now." St. Colman, therefore, by superior learning and piety, and, perhaps, by having been instrumental in converting the Saxons in the North, became eventually their archbishop.

been prescribed by St. John,* *whose disciples had been founders of the Irish Church.* I marvel," he exclaimed, "how some can call that absurd, in which we follow the example of so great an Apostle, one who was thought worthy of reposing on the bosom of his Lord : and can it be believed that such men as our venerable father Columkill, and his successors, would have thought or acted contrary to the precepts of the Sacred Scriptures ?"

The Council, however, decided against St. Colman, who resigned the See of York and returned to Ireland. From this it is clear what was the belief of an Irish bishop, so early as the seventh century, with respect to the introduction of the Church into Ireland. This is sufficient to prove to us that the Cornish Church, strengthened as it was from Ireland, must have been in observance of Eastern customs, and consequently in communion with the Eastern Church.

Now, we have monuments still remaining in Cornwall, Wales, and Ireland which bear the

---

* It is remarkable that in several parts of Ireland seven churches are found built near to each other. A pious modern writer expresses his belief, " that this number seven was chosen in humble imitation and remembrance of the Seven Primitive Churches mentioned in the Revelations, which book was written by the great Apostle of the early saints of Ireland, St. John." There were seven collegiate establishments in Cornwall in early times, of which that in honour of St. Piran was one.

stamp and character of the Eastern Church.
These certainly must place beyond doubt the
character of the Cornish Church as compared
with the Saxon : and, in point of antiquity, refer
themselves to a period anterior to the conquest of
Cornwall ; for the Saxons shew little sign of any
conciliating spirit, such as that, for instance, which
Pope Gregory urged his missionaries to observe
towards them, in not destroying their heathen
temples, but converting them to sacred purposes
of a true religion. It cannot be supposed that
the Saxons, who carried on a war of extermi-
nation ; who always sought to overcome by force
of arms, and never by persuasion ; who, even
when converted to Christianity, sought, if anything, more eagerly to abolish the rites and discipline of the Eastern Church ; — it cannot be
supposed that these or their successors would
ever have adopted any sign or custom which was
a mark of another branch of the Church, and
already in use among their enemies.

The monuments, then, which remain to this
day in Cornwall, of the Eastern Church, and
which we venture to pronounce to be British,
consist of *Crosses.*

Cornwall, Wales, and Ireland abound with
" wayside" and " churchyard" crosses ; and it
is a remarkable fact, which seems to have escaped
notice, that all these, with a very few exceptions
indeed, are Greek crosses ; that is, having four

short equal limbs. They are, in general, carved
upon granite, or formed by four holes pierced
through the block, and all fully attest, by their
venerable and rounded appearance, that they are
of ancient date. The most ancient of these are
of a memorial character, and bear Roman-British
names, surmounted with a Greek cross, rudely cut
upon a long block of hewn granite, such as the
Druids used for forming their circles. These may
fairly be attributed to the fourth or fifth century,
and were erected before cemeteries were in general
use ; for they are found, like the cairns or tumuli
of the heathen British chiefs, upon hills and
downs and other conspicuous places.

Two of the best of these interesting monuments
are at present, unfortunately, not so much respected as they should be. They are indeed the
most ancient ecclesiastical remains in England,
but few seem to regard them ; one serves as a
gate-post to a vicarage in the neighbourhood of
Truro ; the other, if not destroyed, lies neglected
by the roadside near Fowey.

But the greater number of crosses in this
county are of somewhat later date than these, and
not so rude in appearance, though rude enough to
be attributed to a period anterior to the conquest
of Cornwall, when the British Church flourished
there in independence. They consist mostly of a
single shaft of granite, surmounted with a disc, in
which a cross of four equal limbs is carved in

bold relief or sunk into the surface. Sometimes
the limbs are bound by a circle, the intermediate
spaces being pierced ; and some few are formed by
four holes arranged crosswise, and perforated
through the disc, as the cross of St. Piran, of
which we give a representation at page 25. In
the western parts of the county, instead of a cross,
the disc bears a rude sculpture of a human figure,
with arms extended. Every parish in Cornwall
contains several crosses ; and almost every churchyard has one at least, which is often raised on a
mound or steps, and always on the *south side* of
the church, facing the west. Besides this, others
are frequently found, sometimes on the wayside,
and sometimes used as boundary-stones or landmarks in different parts of the parish.

The rude and venerable appearance of these
crosses fully confirms the antiquity which their
Greek character assigns to them ; nor is there, generally speaking, any moulding or other feature
upon them which would lead one to attribute
them to a later date.

Another peculiarity of the early Eastern Church,
common to Cornwall and Wales, where the rites
and discipline of that branch of the Church Catholic were retained longest, is observable in the
names of parishes. In accordance with an Eastern
custom, the British denominated a district which
contained a church, by the name of the tutelary
saint in honour of whom that church was dedi-

cated. Hence the striking difference which exists between British and Saxon names.

This peculiar and distinctive custom prevailed here, and had been established some time before the reign of Edward the Confessor, A.D. 1030; and it is not improbable that it was adopted throughout Britain during the government of the Romans, as early as the beginning of the fourth century. The name of St. Alban, in Hertfordshire, is to this day a monument of the place of his martyrdom. After the Diocletian persecution, when the conversion of Constantine brought rest and protection to the Church, a church was built in memory of this British martyr,* which was standing in the time of Venerable Bede, three hundred years after. Indeed, so general was the custom, at this period, of building churches over the graves of martyrs, confessors, and others, to perpetuate their name, that Eusebius, and other writers of this age, use the term "martyry," and others similar to it, in their accounts of these churches. Eusebius records of Constantine, that he adorned his new city, Constantinople, with many oratories and ample *martyries*. Socrates speaks of the martyry of Thomas the Apostle, in Edessa; the martyry of

* Offa, King of Mercia, founded an abbey on the site of the original Roman-British church in honour of St. Alban, but not before the *British* had been canonized at Rome into an English martyr.

Euphemia, when the Great Council of Chalcedon was held, and many others. Though St. Alban's is almost the only name which has reached our times, there cannot then be a doubt that the British Church furnished other martyrs, for the sake of the Gospel, in the same persecution, whose memory was also honoured. Gildas, our oldest historian, tells us that the Diocletian persecution " caused many churches to be destroyed, particularly in Britain. But the Christians built them up again, new from the ground, when the persecution was over, and founded others besides, to be so many *memorials and trophies* of their martyrs." These churches were again destroyed by the Saxons in the next century; and the names of holy martyrs, whom they were intended to perpetuate, are lost with them. St. Alban's church and name seem alone[*] to have survived the general wreck of the British Church in the central parts of England; and under the circumstances are a strong evidence of the antiquity of the British custom of calling places by the names of the holy men.

Other traces of the Eastern Church in Cornwall, we shall refer to hereafter; those which have been adduced are sufficient to prove that the British

---

[*] It is not improbable that the words "kirk," "church," " circ," forming a part of the name of a place, indicate the site of some of these destroyed churches; as the word " boro'," and " brough," &c. that of a burrow of a British chieftain.

Church flourished here, retaining its peculiarities for centuries before and after the conversion of the Saxons, and that there are remains in Cornwall which bear testimony to this fact.

Antiquities may always be regarded as useful and interesting, not only in confirming points of history, but also as an index of the character of the period they represent. The early ecclesiastical remains in Cornwall confirm all that we can desire, and possess every character which we should seek, in the representatives of the age to which we attribute them. The marked and decided differences which we have traced between the British and the Saxons, especially in ecclesiastical matters, are not imaginary or exaggerated. They will bear investigation, and even repay the trouble. It is surprising that the histories of our Church should have passed them over in silence.

It is obvious, then, as we said before, that rules and theories of architecture, which are founded upon Saxon authority, and derived from Saxon sources, cannot be applicable to the early antiquities of this country. And in applying this remark to St. Piran's Church, it must be urged, that all prejudiced opinions of its date, especially those which are derived from the Saxons, must be laid aside. In short, Saxon prejudices must be forgotten, or be set at defiance. As of old, the Cornish defied the Saxons, and would not submit to their innovation and arbitrary laws; so must the Cornish antiquary, while one stone remains carved or uncarved, maintain his ground, protesting ;—but away with this dream of contention! Antiquaries, and those who love antiquities, are not Saxon, they are peaceful and believing, ever delighted to find, and ready to receive, a relic of other days, willing rather to believe than disbelieve ; they seek not proofs alone, probabilities are sufficient. And herein is a virtue others will do well to imitate. It is better and wiser to believe than disbelieve, even when we cannot comprehend. Let this be the rule of our lives, and we shall find not only that we gain far more by believing than we can lose, but that it is a humble and healthier state of mind. The ridicule which the world may think fit to bestow on the " credulous" is but trifling, and not to be compared to the benefit and pleasure even of believing too much.

The probabilities upon which the claims of this Church to British antiquity rest, are these : without a single evidence or mark of later date, every probability suggests that it was erected soon after St. Piran's death, over his resting-place. It possesses in itself every indication of British antiquity ; is situated among antiquities of a yet remoter age ; has been preserved, perhaps, in the only way in which it could have been preserved, beneath sand. Buried and lost, it has been the subject of tradition from time immemorial ; tradi-

tion has even pointed to the place of its sepulture;
there, in that place, it is at length found.   Upon
examination, it proves to correspond with models
which we derive from the writings of earliest fathers and historians; and, differing from Saxon
and Norman structures, it corresponds exactly
with those which were built by the Irish missionaries, both here and in their own country, and
elsewhere.   Upon these probabilities we venture
to ask for the oratory of St. Piran an early British
antiquity.

PERRAN-ZABULOE.

CHAPTER I.

ST. PERRAN, or Perran-zabuloe, is a large and extensive parish on the north coast of Cornwall. It is situated about six miles from the ancient borough of Truro, on the western part of the Hundred of Pyder, originally called Rialton. The name of this parish, like that of many others in Cornwall, Wales, and Ireland, and the few adjacent islands, is derived, or rather adopted, from its patron saint ; a circumstance which bespeaks British antiquity, and, as we have seen before, is some evidence of the Eastern observances of the Church in these parts. It is worthy of remark, that, with very few exceptions indeed, the names of parishes thus adopted, are the names of holy Confessors, or Martyrs, who were members of the Eastern Church, or some other in communion with it, during the time that the controversy between the Latin and Greek branches of the Ca-

tholic Church, especially in this country, prevailed in its greatest extent. The names of places
founded by the Saxons, on the other hand, are
different in character as in derivation. They are
of a secular character, and derived not from the
Church in any way, but from some local circumstance, such as the proximity of a castle, or forti-
fication, or encampment, or of a river, or wood, or
valley, and the like. This seems also to have
been the custom of the Britons at a very remote
period, probably before their conversion. To this
day Celtic names thus derived remain, and are in
use. Every hill, and valley, and plain, has its
own appropriate appellation, but all these are
now merged into that of the patron saint, and
have been so for many centuries. Each com-
munity,—for at that time parishes had not been
divided as they are at the present,*— however its
members were scattered in various places of different name, as to their spiritual interests they
were one, associated in one church, known by one

* It is difficult to ascertain how ancient the present division
of parishes is. It seems agreed on all hands that in the early
ages of Christianity in this island parishes were unknown, or at
least signified the same that *diocese* does now. Camden says,
England was divided into parishes by Archbishop Honorius
about the year 630. But Selden has clearly shewn that the
clergy lived in common, without any division of parishes, long
after the time mentioned by Camden. It appears, however,
rom the Saxon laws, that parishes were in being long before
the date of the Council of Lateran, A.D. 1179.

name, that of their tutelary saint, in honour of
whom their sanctuary was dedicated to the service of God. Indeed, so far was this carried, that
each district was identified, in terms at least, with
its church. The names the early British Christians gave to their respective districts, we find to
be composed of that of the patron saint, with the
Celtic word " Lan" prefixed to it, thus : " Lanpiran," the church of St. Piran ; Lan-probus, and
many others.* In the Domesday Book of William
the Conqueror, all Cornish parishes which bear
indication of British origin, are thus named, with
only one solitary exception, which is written
" St. Wenn." At present, however, only fourteen
or fifteen *parishes* preserve their original title,
though many villages still retain a name prefixed with "Lan," where all other traces of the
church from which it was derived are gone.
These we may suppose, at the time parishes were
divided, were too small, or, in other respects,
not eligible enough to be converted into a parish,
and were accordingly included under some other,
and in their subordinate position have declined
and passed away ; so that no traces of the church,
or even, in most cases, of its consecrated pre-

* Sometimes the word " Lan" is prefixed to a term of
locality, as Lamborne, that is, Lan-bron, " a church on an
enclosed hill," in this parish. In this village, Lyson says,
"there was a chapel," and very lately some traces of it have
been discovered.

cincts are now found, only the name beginning
with " Lan" remains to indicate where once there
was a British church.

The first record which has reached our times,
with the mention of this parish under its present
altered name, is the will of Sir John Arundel, of
Trerice, dated 1433. In this the original " Lanpiran " is superseded by the lengthy and eupho-
nous " Sanctus Pyeranus-in-zabulo;" which, contracted, so to say, to its present length, Perran-
zabuloe, remains the appellation of the parish of
which we are treating. Before we leave the subject of derivation, it may be permitted to notice
the word " Zabuloe," which has been appended to
Perran. As part of a Cornish name, it is singular
on account of its Latin derivation : and its adop-
tion, too, was unnecessary, that is, for the purposes of distinction ; for the two other parishes
called after the same saint, from the earliest
times have been distinguished from this by appropriate Celtic names, " Arworthal," and " Uth-
noe."

The word zabuloe is derived from sabulum, fine
sand, and was, doubtless, added in allusion to the
destructive element which had overwhelmed the
sanctuary and burial-place of St. Piran ; for at
the time it was adopted, that is, at any time
before 1433, the date of the will already referred
to, it could have been applicable but to a very
small portion of this large parish, that, namely,

which contained the venerated relics of its patron saint.

The neighbourhood in which Perran-zabuloe is situated, may fairly be affirmed to have been important and populous, if not at a remote period before, at least during, the fifth century, when St. Piran came hither. The numerous British and Roman antiquities which are frequently found here, fully justify the assertion, although the desolate and uninviting appearance of some of the hills and downs may lead one to entertain a different impression.

The antiquities referred to, consist of rude implements of husbandry, called " celts," and weapons of war, such as arrow and spear heads, and axes, all made of flint and sharpened stones, (though some few are of metal,) and of fragments of pottery, both of the British and the Romans, and coins of the latter. Besides these, which we may suppose had been hidden from the sight of men for many centuries, there are other remains which our ancestors looked upon in their day, and spared to us, that we, too, should do likewise for posterity. These are " hill-castles," (cäerdinas,) of which there were not less than four within sight of each other in the north and eastern parts of the parish. An amphitheatre, or Cornish Round, where in early times, when men were not capable of higher or more intellectual amusements, they were entertained with feats of strength, such as wrest-

ling, for which the Cornish are still famous, and
hurling, and other sports. And lastly, sepulchral
mounds, or burrows, where the ashes of the chieftains of ancient times were deposited. Of these
there are a great number in this parish; almost
every hill is marked by one at least, and many
of them by more. All these bespeak an over-
flowing population at a remote period : they tell
of a place where people dwelt, where they were
entertained in their simplicity ; of a place which
was worthy of defence when invaders threatened to
take possession of it or to destroy it; and of a place,
moreover, which was endeared to its inhabitants
by the sepulchral mounds of their departed chieftains and warriors. They tell of all these, and
even more. Their ruined and despoiled condition
attest that our age has not fulfilled the trust
which our fathers for generations have preserved
to us. They spared these monuments of other
days ; as they received, so they transmitted them :
but we have not done so ; we have not regarded
posterity, as we have been regarded of old. There
is scarcely a single monument of the British times
which has not been subjected to the test of our
curiosity, or "research," as it is termed. All indicate the same selfish disregard of posterity, and
the rationalistic spirit, which is the curse and
stigma of our age. Such is the character their
present condition will take down to future generations, of the period when they were destroyed

and plundered. We would refer our remarks especially to the sepulchral burrows around us. It is true, they are but monuments of heathens ; but even this cannot extenuate the evil, even after it has been shewn that Christian remains are respected. There is not a burrow, of all the many which the piety and respect for the dead of former times has spared, which has not been searched, and plundered, and left in ruin ; and almost all of them within the memory of man, and all certainly within the last century.

They were reared fourteen or fifteen centuries ago, as a mark of respect and honour, over the ashes of beloved and esteemed chieftains. It was for such a monument as this that they undertook deeds of danger,—the brief immortality of fame and time was all they knew,—for this they fought, and bled, and died. It was the dying hope, as it had been the aim and attainment of their lives, to be remembered in the sepulchral mound, that their name should be handed down to posterity, and their deeds the subject of the songs of bards and minstrels. " Fall I may," forebodes the gloomy chieftain of Carricthura ; " but raise my tomb, Crimora. Grey stones and a mound of earth shall send my name to other times." And again, " If fall I must in the field, raise high my grave, Vinvela. Grey stones and heaped up earth shall mark me to future times. When the hunter shall sit down by the mound

and produce his food at noon, 'Some warrior rests
here,' he will say, and my fame shall live on in his
praise.   Remember me, Vinvela, when low in the
earth." *   Such were the hopes of their lives, and
their poor consolation in death.   Christians, however, have been who have respected them ; but it
has remained for the enlightened times in which
we live to mock these limited hopes, and to tear
down the monument of ages in order to *see* what
was within : as if it were impossible to believe,
impossible to understand, "*how*" warriors were
buried there, without seeing' with our eyes and
handling with our hands.   About a century ago
stood a large burrow on Lamborne Downs, in the
vicinity of the Hill Castles already referred to,
called " Creeg mear," or the Great Mound.   This,
in order to save a trifling expense, was opened in
search of stone for a hedge by a labouring man.
The mound being of earth, he found none, except
three or four large stones, which were arranged in
the form of a " Kist-Vaen," or stone chest.   Within this he discovered nine urns, which he immediately broke ; but, to his disappointment, they
contained only ashes.

* Though the genuineness of M'Pherson's " Ossian" may
be justly doubted, the authenticity of the passages quoted, as
far as regards our argument, is fully borne out by comparison
with fragments of poems which remain in Ireland and Scotland, and which are allowed to be genuine.   From these it
appears that M'Pherson's "Ossian" was more a plagiarism
than an original composition.

Thus were this burrow and its time-honoured contents destroyed ; a field, called the "Burrow Field" to this day, marks its site. But it is not by the hand of the ignorant labourer alone that these sepulchres of the chieftains of ages past have been rifled and desecrated. The educated, the learned, the professed lovers of antiquity,— shame that it must be said,—have helped to tear up these venerable remains of antiquity ; what is worse, they glory in the desecration, and bear away the frail urn in triumph to grace some library or museum ! As if they had been spared by countless generations only for our gratification, as objects to exercise our research, in order that we should gratify our desire and surpassing love for antiquities, or rather, it must be said, our wanton and profane curiosity. How is it, that ages we are accustomed to denounce as "dark and superstitious" with utmost complacency, shew more piety, more religious regard for the dead ? and if for heathen dead, much more for those who rest in consecrated ground. We may learn much from our ancestors of old, whom we affect to despise, and should not be ashamed to acknow- ledge it. With all their errors, the monuments of their time, and those which they have transmitted to us, all indicate a generous and disinterested piety and religious tone of mind, which we do not possess yet. " They dreamed not of a perishable home," their thoughts were not confined to themselves or to their own generation, but their thoughts and deeds were to God and for posterity. Their precept and their example were the blessings

> " We from our fathers have received in trust,
> We to our children will transmit, and die ;
> This is our maxim, this our piety,
> And God and nature own that it is just."

Such were their thoughts to usward: however they were deluded and lost in superstitions,—however wandering in error,—they built, they planted, they preserved, and all for posterity. This was their character compared with ours. The huge and conspicuous monuments of early days around us attest and confirm this character—their "maxim and their piety," and to future generations they will attest it ; but of us, in their despoiled and ruined condition, they will attest of our age,—the age in which they were destroyed,—that we cared not for posterity as we had been cared for of old. Monuments they were of the piety of those who spared them ; monuments they are, and will be to future generations, of the selfish and profane curiosity which has destroyed them.

But to return. These antiquities which we have enumerated, the memorials of a period wrapped in darkness, they shew us where generations and generations of our fellow-men fought and bled, where in peaceful times they were entertained, and where at length they were "consigned to earth;" but they can tell us no more. They belong to an era settled in gloom, which no record can reach, and no ingenuity penetrate. But it is enough for our purpose that they were the resort of multitudes, that the scenes among which they are situated were once peopled by a benighted race, whose pleasures, like their hopes, were confined to earth,—limited and perishing.

Among these scenes St. Piran, the messenger of God, came to a rude and uncultivated race,—a light to them that sate in darkness. He came with the glad tidings of the Gospel, to teach more lasting joys, and to implant in their breasts loftier and more enduring hopes of immortality. He was not the first: many before him had worked for the sake of the Gospel, had braved dangers and endured hardships, persecutions, and even death. The faint and glimmering records of early times tell of persecutions and martyrdoms. But who were these martyrs and confessors? Who these messengers of God, who suffered at the hands of their fellow-creatures,—came to impart inestimable blessings, but suffered? Their names and their deeds are alike unknown? They rest from their labours and are in peace, and their deeds are recorded where they cannot be effaced or forgotten.

With the same gracious purpose and holy zeal as his predecessors, St. Piran entered upon his

labours in the vineyard so fraught with danger ;
but only temporal danger, and capable of lasting
and enduring rewards.

The site he fixed upon for his humble dwelling
we may regard as characteristic of his earnestness
in the work to which he had devoted himself.
The sand which had concealed the spot for centuries, now removed, discloses that it was in a
retired valley by the sea-shore, yet within sight
of the amphitheatre, the general resort of the
inhabitants. Here, in retirement and loneliness,
he prayed for success with faith and confidence.
Here he watched his opportunity to further his
pious intentions, and went forth to the haunts of
men, .with peaceful steps and unoffending words,
to entreat them to turn from vanities to the
living God. We know his prayers were not in-
effectual, or his efforts vain. A little spring
welled up beside his lowly dwelling. Here, we
may presume, he baptized those whom God had
given him. At this spring, which remains to this
day, he received his converts, and admitted them
to the privileges which the Redeemer of Mankind
had purchased for them ; assuring them of that
pardon, and rest, and glory, and immortality which
remain for the people of God. To what extent
his labours were blessed during his life, we have
no means of knowing. It is not always that the
servants of the Lord are permitted, in this world,
to reap the fruit of their labour ; "one soweth,

and another reapeth." Only to a few is it granted, in fulfilment of their fondest and long-cherished hopes, to exclaim with the gratitude, and in the words of the holy Simeon, "Lord, now lettest Thou thy servant depart in peace." The brief records of that portion of his life which was passed in Cornwall, tell us of a *few* who attended him at his departure, and that they buried him beside the place where he had dwelt. The narrative states, " that, worn out with age and infirmity, he called his converts, his children in the spirit, around him; and, having exhorted them for the last time, he commanded his grave to be prepared, and, descending into it with calmness, his spirit departed.

Modern research has torn down the altar-tomb which once stood over St. Piran's remains — and " investigation" confirms the narrative. There is no kist-vaen, or stone chest, but merely the sandy bed wherein the holy bishop rests in peace. Who will venture to say, that an oratory* was not erected over his precious remains, according to the custom of the time? Who will venture to deny, that that oratory is not the same which is now disclosed to view, but, as if only to be utterly destroyed? But of this hereafter.

The events which we have been contemplating

* Oratory, derived from οἶκοι εὐκτήριοι, the houses of prayer, is a term used for a church at a very early period. In those days, as now, the church was especially a house of prayer.

are as a dream; the scene of them, long centuries
ago, was removed from human sight. Deluges
of sand, which from time to time have been
poured upon this devoted spot and its vicinity,
have overwhelmed not only this, but another
church besides. At first, the sand gathered round
the humble oratory of St. Piran, and threatening to
overwhelm it, advanced to a river which flowed
eastward of the church, along the middle of the
valley, or "coomb," to the sea. Here, as if by
"secret antipathy," it could not cross; and, ac-
cumulating into a vast hill, the submersion of
the oratory of St. Piran was completed. But so
effectually was the progress of the devastation
restrained by the stream, that the inhabitants,
unwilling to remove far from the burial-place
of St. Piran, their tutelary saint, erected another
edifice to his memory, about the same distance
from the stream, but on the opposite side. It
may appear difficult to understand how a narrow
stream kept back mountains of loose light sand:
but it matters not *how*, the fact is certain; history and antiquities confirm that for centuries
it did so; and it was not till the course of the
stream had been turned, and the water had been
drawn off by the workings of a mine in the neighbourhood, that the sand, at last, again began its
work of desolation. So secure, indeed, was the
second church so late as the year 1420, that, like
almost every church in Cornwall, this was rebuilt in

the style of the period on a magnificent scale. Full a century it continued free of danger from the sand ; but, after that, all historians agree in their report of the devastation and desolation which had begun. In the end of the sixteenth century Carew writes, " This parishe too well brookyth his name ' in sabulo ;' for the light sande carried up by the North-(west ?) wind daily continueth his covering and marring the lands adjoynant." Borlase, in the middle of the last century, briefly notes, "the second church is in no small danger." Such was the rapidity with which the sand accumulated, that parishioners still alive remember when, during the winter, it has been blown against the side of the church, so as to bury the porch entirely in one night. The inconvenience and troublesome nature of the sand at length compelled the inhabitants, though reluctantly, to remove their church from the destruction which threatened it. Accordingly, in the year 1803, it was resolved—by no means unanimously—to take down the church and rebuild it elsewhere. The tower, windows, arches and pillars, and the porch, were accordingly removed to a distance of two miles, and again erected at a part of the parish called Lamborne.

A solitary granite cross, and three roughly-piled hillocks of stone, (over the graves of members of a family who still bury, and desire to be buried, among the ruins,) mark the site of the

second church. The sand is nineteen feet above
the floor of the church; and, now that its work
of spoliation is completed, it seems at rest, a rich
turf covers its surface, and sheep pasture where
once suffocating clouds of sand were whirled aloft
in reckless fury. As if the minister of some
evil spirit of destruction, its work being done—it
rests ; but beyond this ruin, in the north and
east, the sands may still be seen, like the tem-
pestuous ocean, blown about by every wind, and
whirled up into grotesque points and hills—a
wild and desolate scene! Not a blade of grass
or any verdure meets the eye, save here and there
a few tufts of the coarse " sea-bent," through
which the wind moans and sighs as it passes
over the desolate region. The wild scene presents hills and valleys and undulating swells,
smooth, solitary, and desolate.

At the northern extremity of the sands, about
a mile from the second church, it may still be
seen how a narrow stream keeps back mountains
and mountains of loose sand. Here glides the
little stream peacefully to the sea,—between a
green field, where cattle graze in security, on the
one side, and the wildest imaginable scene on the
other ; a cliff of loose sand, full one hundred feet
high, overhangs the stream, and cannot cross.
Such, we may imagine, was the scene at the
former stream before the destruction of the second
church. For at least three centuries the sands

have overhung the stream at Helenglaze; and while the water flows on, as now, it will never go beyond : however it may swell, and tempests whirl it aloft in fury, its boundary is fixed, *which it must not and cannot pass.*

But let us return to the oratory of St. Piran. Centuries have elapsed,—the shifting nature of these sands discloses the long lost relic of other days. Once it slept beneath a lofty hill; and now, behold a valley—and a lake! Human efforts have hastened the work of exhumation. In 1835 the sanctuary was restored, perfect as the day in which it was overwhelmed. There, too, was the spring, the well of St. Piran, and his baptistery : the sand has choked its course; and in the winter, when it swells, the water forms a lake, and rises within the church to the height of six feet. Accordingly for eight or nine months in the year the floor and seats of the church are under water, and always under sand, for it is impossible to keep it out. Beside the baptistery is a little rude cell, a few yards to the south-east of the church. The words of Spenser do not inaptly describe the group before us :

" A litle lowly hermitage it was,
    Downe in a dale,——
    Far from resort of people, that did pas
    In traveill to and fro : a litle wyde
    There was a holy chappell edifyde,
    Wherein the hermite dewly wont to say
    His holy things each morn and eventyde :

Thereby a chrystall streame did gently play,
Which from a sacred fountaine welled forth a way."
SPENCER, Book I. c. 34.

The church, we have said, in 1835—nay, till
1838—was perfect; but how is it now changed,
despoiled, and wantonly torn down! It presents
but a wreck of what it was even a few years ago;
a sad spectacle, which is not relieved by the remains of mortality that surround it. Long after
this church was overwhelmed, hundreds were
buried in the hill which covered it, in preference
to the cemetery of the second church. The remains of all these have been scattered to the
winds. Gilbert, who visited this spot thirty
years since, thus describes the melancholy scene :
" On the south side is the burial-ground, where
there are scattered thousands of teeth and other
human bones. Even whole skeletons lie exposed,
in regular order; and, strange as it may appear,
the showers of sand that are continually wafted
over this desolate spot scarcely ever alight on
these melancholy relics of mortality." Hundreds
and hundreds of skeletons have been exposed—
destroyed by the shifting of the sands. The valley
is full of remnants of bones and teeth; they
whiten the sand round the church; and, instead
of commanding some pity and regard, they seem
but to incite visitors to tear up more, which are
too easily found, so plentiful are they; and they
are torn up from their resting-place of ages, to

gratify mere wanton curiosity. Often disjoint-
ed in the attempt, they are left scattered on the
surface of the sand, dishonoured and insulted—
a sad spectacle in a Christian land.

The little ruined church, the uptorn graves,
the neglected and dishonoured remains of poor
mortality, which are strewed about in that lonely
valley, all speak too clearly that it is not the
gentle and silent hand of Time alone which has
been doing the work of spoliation ; but a more
active and a more ruthless enemy. With just
indignation at the sad scene, we cannot but
exclaim in the words of the poet of Cooper's
Hill,

> " Who sees these dismal heaps, but will demand
> What barbarous invader sack'd the land ?
> But when he hears, no Goth, no Turk did bring
> This desolation——
> While nothing but the name of zeal appears
> 'Twixt our best actions and the worst of theirs—
> What must he think our sacrilege would spare,
> If such the effects of our devotion are ?"

and not exclaim in vain ! For there are some
who respect that sacred spot ;—there are some
who look with sorrow upon this scene of unhallowed spoliation,—who could never put forth
their hand to despoil this consecrated place of
ages, or dare to desecrate the place where Christians worshipped, and where Christians rest, —
and who, moreover, could never find gratification

in disturbing the time-honoured remains of the
sacred dead.

If we would but reflect on the subject, there
is much—very much—which ought to have preserved this ancient oratory and its hallowed precincts, and preserved them in veneration. There is
much which ought to protect them even now,
despoiled as they are, from further desecration.
There are associations connected with that holy
spot, which claim for it our regard and protection. It is true, the general appearance of this
church has nothing in it to recommend it to our
admiration, particularly in its present ruinous
condition, despoiled and broken down as it is,
and half buried in sand. It has little to win
for it the admiration of the stranger, much less,
indeed, than most ruins; all of which add so much
interest, and so many charms, to the beauty of
our native scenery : but this little sanctuary
possesses features of interest, surpassing those of
beauty, which speak not to the senses, but to the
heart ; which speak not to those who must see
and handle for themselves, but to those who *think*
and *believe.*

Connected as it is with the early history of our
Church, it should be interesting to every Englishman, and not the less so as a monument of those
primitive times when the Church first began its
troubled existence in this country. That Church,
be it remembered, which, notwithstanding all the

persecutions and trials to which it was subjected, has proved the blessing, safeguard, and advancement of our country above all countries : for it is not our arm or our strength that hath delivered us ; but God, for the sake of His holy Church, has advanced our state among the nations of the world.

As of old the Lord blessed the lone widow who entertained His prophet, so that her cruse of oil failed not, neither her barrel of meal, in the time of famine ; so has the same Lord blessed our land with His holy Church, and for her sake. Can we then in justice, in reason, or in gratitude, boast of our position, and forget the cause of our advancement ? Our forefathers thought not so : the monuments of their gratitude for the spiritual and temporal blessings showered upon this land are around us on every side. The almost sole monuments of their wealth, and skill, and industry, remain in their churches and magnificent cathedrals; and all dedicated, with piety, to their God.

> " The temples of His grace,
> How beautiful they stand ;
> The honours of our native place,
> The bulwarks of our land !"

These indicate what is true patriotism ; that it should be, as it was of old, built upon the Church of God :—surely every Englishman should prize and esteem the things connected with the

Church. In this light should he regard with
interest this little edifice of other days, and protect it as a national relic.

Besides this, is it not interesting to look upon
a memorial of a remote age, disclosed directly to
us from most ancient times ? Intermediate generations have but preserved and handed down
its memory to us, without seeing it. After a
lapse of perhaps a thousand years, we behold the
structure once more disclosed to view. And
again.— Can we look upon those rudely-built
walls, and feel no interest in the simple piety of
those who reared them?—piety we are bound to
say; for it is not only unjust to the memory of
our primitive brethren, but inconsistent with
their character, to suppose they did not give their
best and first efforts of their skill and industry
—the best offering within their reach—to their
God :—this is especially the character of the age.
Rude as those walls are, there is still an effort
apparent in their structure, which marks them as
the work of a simple people who did their best.
Even their rudeness and simplicity, therefore,
command our esteem, and should engage some
interest.

But there are higher and holier thoughts connected with that humble and unpretending ruin.
It has been consecrated to the service of the High
God. In it our own brethren, servants of the
same Master, called by the same baptism to the

same privileges and hopes,—in it they worshipped in simplicity as simple as their oratory; and, it may be, they worshipped in many of the very forms and the very words we are still permitted to use to this day! Long, long may the blessed privilege remain to our favoured land; and may that day speedily come, when all England's sons and daughters, united in one fold, shall utter with heart and voice the same pure and Scriptural form of words which are, and have been so long, our national blessing and our national privilege!

There, in that sanctuary, our fellow Christians prayed, and gave thanks; and, when their day of trial was past, they were consigned to the hallowed precincts, there to rest till time shall be no more. The faithful dead were "committed to the ground" centuries and centuries ago around that humble house of prayer: they were deposited there in pious hope that they would be suffered to rest in peace. Is it not a monstrous act of profanation, unworthy the name and profession of a Christian, to drag them forth for no purpose but to gratify curiosity? Is it not an impious and unholy deed?—can there be gratification in it? Oh, let them rest in peace! they hallow more that hallowed spot—that wild and lonely place, where Christians rest. Surely, then, there are associations and recollections connected with this little sanctuary, and its sacred precincts, which command our respect and reverence, even

E

if we can feel no interest. Surely there are only
a very, very few, if any, who possess not some
better and kindlier feelings of piety, to discoun-
tenance such unhallowed and profane desecration.
It is not because human laws punish not the unholy deed, that it may be done with impunity.
Human laws can reach it,—piety must denounce
it. But there is another consequence which must
inevitably follow; for no mortal ever did, and
ever will, mock the sacred things of God with
impunity!

Is it a wonder that so many are found to slight
the ordinances of the Lord, and to denounce the
truths and doctrines of the Church as superstitions, when sense of piety and regard for the dead
are at so low an ebb? Is it a wonder that so
many are incapable of appreciating the beautiful
and harmonious system of the Church, especially
in this devoted county, when they make no distinction between consecrated and unconsecrated,
who for amusement can dare to disinter the remains of departed Christians? Heretics and
apostates are honoured in their unconsecrated
graves; but the dead of pure and primitive
times are dishonoured! This is no exaggerated
statement, but sadly applicable to an undiscri-
minating age; though it may be extenuated a
little by the plea of thoughtlessness and ignorance. For there are many who would not wil-
fully and wantonly deface or despoil a church,

and much less rifle the tombs around it ; but
who, nevertheless, think nothing of " digging in
the sands to find a skeleton," or, perhaps, to see
for themselves the manner of ancient sepulture.
They little deem that the remains they disinter
are those of Christians, deposited in consecrated
ground ; they little think it is a most unhallowed deed, and most unholy gratification which can
arise from it.

It is but just to add, that, in the majority of
cases, the desecration complained of may be im-
puted to the vague and indistinct notions which
are entertained with respect to the religion of
early times. It has truly been said, " the history
of the Church of England has too often been
written as if it had been nothing but superstition on the one side, and imposture on the other ;"
and the general opinion of the world seems un-
thinkingly to have acquiesced in this. The term
" Christianity" is vaguely applied to it ; a term
which is also, in the liberality of the age, applied
to every shade and denomination of heresy. But,
in truth, it is a serious word to trifle with ; it
is not ours to do as we will with it, or to place
upon it what interpretation we please. Applied
to the religion of past, or present, or future times,
it has one definite meaning,—it is the religion of
Christ ; that religion which He established on
earth, with its perpetual ordinances and ministry ;
which has His Almighty promise that " the

gates of Hell shall not prevail against it," and
the assurance that "He will be with it to the
end of the world." All whom interest or curiosity has led to the oratory of St. Piran, have not
regarded it as the sacred relic it is. It has been
destroyed because they thought not, and did not
realize to their mind, that it was a consecrated
structure; and that the sacred dead who rest beside it were churchmen and Christians—the servants of Christ, who abide His second coming.

CHAPTER II.

BEFORE we come to a description of the oratory of St. Piran as it was when first recovered from the sands in the year 1835, let us dwell for a brief space on the life of the saint in honour of whom it was dedicated to God.

St. Piranus, called in Ireland Kyeranus, was born, according to Camden and Archbishop Ussher, about the middle of the fourth century, in the province of Ossory in Ireland. His parents were of noble birth, by name Domuel and Wingela; the latter of whom, his mother, accompanied him to Cornwall, and founded a monastery in the neighbourhood of her son's dwelling, and it is supposed lies buried beside him in the oratory in the sands. Piranus lived to the age of "thirty years without baptism," and, having received some imperfect knowledge of the Christian faith by the conversation of certain laics, took a journey to Rome, in order to be instructed in the heavenly doctrine and learn faithfully to practise its precepts. At Rome he remained twenty years, diligently studying the Holy Scriptures, and was baptized. Up to the end of the fourth century, although Christianity had been some time introduced into Ireland, it does not appear that it was yet the general religion of the country. Early in the fifth century, when Piranus returned from Rome, St. Patrick had already, with others, entered zealously upon the work of converting his heathen countrymen. Piranus, having received holy orders from St. Patrick, began his ministration in his native province of Ossory. He built himself a cell for his residence," says Butler, "in a place encompassed with woods, near the water of Fueran, which soon grew into a monastery. A town was afterwards built there, called Saigar; now, from the saint, Sîer Kyran. Here he converted to the faith his family and his whole clan, which was that of the Osraigs, with many others. Having given his mother the religious veil, he appointed her a cell or monastery near his own." *

St. Patrick, in the meantime, having been blessed with success in his labours in Cornwall and elsewhere, returned to Ireland, and consecrated twelve bishops to carry on the good work he had been permitted to begin. Among these, Piranus was advanced to the episcopal office, and soon after entered upon his labours in Cornwall. The history of Ireland at this period presents an active scene; the work of conversion and civilization seem to

* A more particular account of his ministrations here are recorded in a work emprynted in the yeare 1500 by De Worde, entitled " Nova Legenda Angliæ."

have been begun simultaneously : the former so
earnestly—such was the zeal and self-denying
piety of the time—that we find even princes and
nobles forsaking crowns and worldly distinctions to
become ministers of the Gospel, and cheerfully undertaking long and tedious journeys to foreign
parts, risking and endangering their lives for the
sake of their high commission. So effectual were
the efforts and example of this century, that
Camden, writing of the next, records, " No men
came up to the Irish monks for sanctity and
learning. They sent forth swarms of holy men
all over Europe, to whom the monasteries of Lux-
uiel in France, Pavia in Italy, Wentzburge in
Froconia, S. Gall in Switzerland, Malmsbury and
Lindisfarne, and many others, owed their origin."
Cornwall may be very appropriately added to this
list.

Piranus, having embarked with his mother and
several other holy women, landed in Cornwall, at
" Pendinas," hill-head, or a head-land, in a place
now known by the name of " St. Ives," from Ia,
one of St. Piran's companions, who appears to
have had some influence in that place. For in the
Legende of St. Ives, contained in the same book
as that of St. Piran, we read that " Tewdor was
king at that time, and had a palace at Pendinas ;
and that Dinan, a greate lorde of Cornwall, at the
request of St. Ia, built a church at the same place."

From hence St. Piran travelled eastward " an

eighteen myles," and took up his abode in a populous district we have already described.   Here he
pursued his ministrations, and did many deeds to
the honour and glory of God.   Nor does it appear
that he confined his labours to this particular district; for there are no less than two other
parishes called after him, and several wells of
"miraculous healing power" in Cornwall.   He
seems also to have gained influence among the
tinners of his time; for to this day he is esteemed,
or rather called, their patron saint, and up to no
remote period St. Piran's day was observed by
them as a festival.*

   At length, however, worn out with age and infirmity, St. Piran called his followers around him, and,
having addressed them for the last time, desired a
grave to be prepared.   He then took leave of
them, and, descending into it with calmness, his
spirit departed on the 5th day of March, about
the year 480.   He rests, continues an old narrative of his life, in Cornwall, on the shore of the
Severn sea, fifteen miles from Petroc-stowe or
Padstow, and twenty-five from Mousehole.†

   * The late Davies Gilbert, Esq. in his interesting History
of Cornwall, states that the banner of St. Piran, a cross argent,
on a field sab. in early times was the armorial ensign of Cornwall.   The present arms of the county, a sab. shield, charged
with thirteen bezants, was the bearing of Robert Earl of Moreton, the brother of William the Conqueror.
   † Two ancient harbours of Cornwall, the former on the
north, and the latter on the south coast.

Nothing can more satisfactorily fix the locality
of St. Piran's resting-place. The several alleged
distances from St. Ives, from Padstow, and Mousehole, each and all bring us to this very place,
which oral tradition has ever pointed to as the
burial-place of St. Piran.

If further evidence be wanting, there is a record
in the Registry at Exeter, which alludes to this
spot as the resort of hundreds of "pilgrims to the
shrine of St. Piran." But there is yet one more
record, which, with certain circumstances connected with it, place beyond doubt that St. Piran was
buried in that very spot where the ancient church
is discovered.

The will of Sir John Arundel of Trerice, which
we have already referred to for the antiquity of
the name of this parish, contains a bequest as
singular as it is useful for our purpose.

"Item, lego ad usum parochie S'c'i Pyerani in
Zabulo ad claudendum capud S. Pierani honorificè
et meliori modo quo sciunt xl. s."

At the time this bequest was made, namely in
the year 1433, the "second church" (which was
taken down forty years ago, and removed to its
present site) had just been completely rebuilt in
the perpendicular style, and in all probability the
head alluded to was enshrined in a niche in the east
wall, behind the high altar.* It is remarkable

* The Vicar of Probus has kindly communicated to the
writer, that, when the chancel of his church was rebuilt, be-

that only the head of St. Piran is mentioned in
the will.

In the year 1835, when the sand was removed
from the "first church," beneath the altar at the
east end three *headless skeletons,* one that of a
woman, probably his mother, were discovered; and
on further examination the heads were found deposited together between the legs of one of the
skeletons, which was lying on the south side of
the altar. The concrete floor of the chancel on
this side had been broken before, as the labourer
employed to remove the altar assures us. These
heads, in all probability, had been enshrined in
the second church, and at the Reformation, when
relics were not regarded with so much reverence
as before, were removed, and again deposited for
safety beneath the chancel of the then lost church,
where it was known St. Piran was buried; for
Camden, who lived after this period, records, "In
sabulo positum Sº. Pirano sacellum ; qui sanctus,
etiam Hibernicus, hìc requiescit." There cannot
remain any doubt, then, of the place of St. Piran's
burial.

History has not handed down the names of his
successors in the ministry ; but, nevertheless, the

hind the altar a niche was discovered, containing two skulls of
different sizes. The church is dedicated in honour of SS.
Probus and Grace, who are buried there. It is not improbable that these were the venerated relics of St. Probus and St.
Grace.

church planted by him in this neighbourhood continued to increase and flourish. In the reign of Edward the Confessor, about the year 1000, (at this time Cornwall had been conquered by the Saxons,) and at least 500 years after St. Piran's time, we find by the Domesday Book that "Lanpiran" was one of seven collegiate establishments in Cornwall. Reference to the extract below will shew the extent of property the church had acquired in the time of William the Conqueror, and that a portion of it was appropriated by the Earl of Moreton, the Conqueror's brother, to whom he had given the dukedom of Cornwall.

CORNUALGE. 121.

Canonici S. Pierani teñ Lanpiran q̃ liƀa fuit T. R. E. Ibi ŝt iij. hidę. T'ra. ē viij. car̃. Ibi ŝt ij. car̃ 7 ij. servi 7 iiij. villi 7 viij. borđ 7 x. ac̃ pasturę. Valet xij. soliđ.

Qđo comes* accepit valeƀ xl. soliđ.

De hoc Maner̃ ablatę ŝt ijᵉ. ꝑrę q̃ reddeƀ canonicis T. R. E firmā iiijᵒʳ. septimanarū 7 decano xx. soliđ p c̃suetudinē.

Harū unā teñ Beruer' de comite Moritoñ 7 de alia hiđ q̃ teñ Odo de S. Pierano abstulit com̃ totā pecuniā.

TERRA COMITIS MORITONIENSIS. 123 b.

Idē† teñ Tregrebri. Eduui teneƀ T. R. E.

_____

* Comes Moritoniensis.   † Ditto.

Ibi ē j. hida q̃ nunq̃ geldaṽ. T'ra ē iij. car̃.
Ibi ē car̃ 7 dimiđ cū j. servo 7 iiij. borđ 7
xxx. ac̃ pasturę. Olī xx. soł. M° vał x.
soliđ.
   H. r̂ra ē de possessione S. Pierañ.

Dugdale's Monasticon, vol. vi. p. 1449, contains
the next account of this place.

In this work notice is taken of the college (unfortunately confused with that at St. Keverne), and
it is recorded that the church was given by Henry
I. to the bishop and church of St. Peter in
Exeter, who still possess the great tithes and ad-
vowson of the vicarage.

Thus have we followed the history of the
church planted by St. Piran in this neighbourhood, to a period comparatively within reach of
more accessible records.

Reverence for the memory of St. Piran, and,
after his burial-place was overwhelmed in the
sand, respect for the place, seem not to have failed
with years, or even centuries. Pilgrims, as we
have seen, resorted to his shrine in great numbers ;
the hill of sand, beneath which his remains were
deposited, long continued to be the favourite
burial-place of the inhabitants ; and, till within
the last fifty years, the Registers of the parish
from the earliest period bear the Christian name
of "Perran," which was transmitted from father
to son ; but now the custom has ceased.

Now, after we have been assured that St. Piran ministered here, and lies buried in the sands, and that the church planted by him has continued in this place for centuries, is it too much to assume that he built an oratory beside his dwelling? It was no unusual deed at his time; three of the holy persons who accompanied him are recorded to have erected churches.

St. Ia, we have seen, had a church erected at her desire. "St. Breage built two churches in the west." "St. Buryan built an oratorie in the same place where she lived." Before St. Piran's time there were monasteries at Padstow, at Bodmin, St. Germains, and at Lanceston.

It is true, the records of the life of St. Piran make no mention of his having erected a church; but it is scarcely consistent with the character of the period, and especially the character of the Irish missionaries, to suppose that they built not churches at every place where they ministered. However, whether St. Piran built an oratory or otherwise, there can be no doubt that the British Christians erected a church; the very name "Lan-piran" implies a British church dedicated in honour of St. Piran. And it is most probable that they erected it over his remains, for it seems impossible to believe that St. Piran had no tomb, no church or altar, dedicated to his memory, when so many holy men of less fame and reputation for piety had theirs.

St. Piran, doubtless, had an oratory and altar
dedicated to him, whether of wood—a wood
wattled with mud—or otherwise, according to the
style, if it may be so called, of the period. The
difficulty still remains ; that is, to prove that this
structure, now discovered, is the same which was
erected immediately after St. Piran's departure
from the world. Let us, however, pass on for the
present : it is hoped in the sequel to shew, from
evidence and examples too, that it is by no means
impossible that the despoiled ruin in the sands
was erected in the sixth century, and overwhelmed about the ninth.

Let us suppose ourselves then in the tenth century : there is great trouble and affliction—the
Saxons are defeating on all sides the determined
and implacable Cornish. The Christians of St.
Piran have hitherto with their countrymen valiant-
ly maintained their liberty and their own peculiar
customs : but other troubles are come upon them ;
the sea has thrown up light sand, which the wind
carries aloft, and threatens therewith to overwhelm
their sanctuary ; in a short time their fears are
realized, the sand by degrees accumulates around
its devoted victim. They are at length reluctantly compelled to dismantle and to desert it. Who
would not grieve to be compelled to give up a
church, in which he and his fathers had worshipped, to certain destruction ? It is overwhelmed
and lost. Still, for centuries, generation after

generation respect the place, and deposit their dead, to rest in peace in its hallowed precincts.*

We will suppose, then, this church buried and lost. Camden, as we have seen, comes first to tell us that there is a church buried in the sand in this neighbourhood, dedicated to St. Perran ; that he was a holy man of Ireland, and that he is buried in it.

Norden, another historian, who lived at the end of the sixteenth century, tells us, " This parish is almost drowned in sea-sande, which the north wind whirleth and driveth to the land in such force that the inhabitantes have been already forced to *move their church*, and yet they are so annoyde as they daily lose their lande." Carew, who follows a few years after, says, " This parish too well brooketh his name Zabulo, for the light sand carried up by the north wind daily continueth his covering and marring the lands adjoynant, so as the distresse of this deluge drave the inhabitantes to remove their church : howbeit, when it meeteth with any crossing brooke, the same by a secret an-

* This may probably have been continued till the Reformation, for the quantity of bones still found is almost incredible : hundreds and thousands must have been buried here. The custom of burying without coffins, but in graves formed of slate-stones placed on their edge, does not render this improbable, for the ancient British custom was continued in many cases till the sixteenth century. See Letter by J. T. Treffry, Esq., to the Royal Institution, Cornwall.

tipathie restraineth and barreth his farder en-
croaching that way."

From both these authors we learn of a church
which is deserted and lost, and of another which
is built on the opposite side of a brook. Neither
of them attempt to describe the forsaken church ;
from which we may infer, as also from the manner
in which they allude to it, that it is still lost, and
that no part of it was at all visible at the time
they wrote. So it continued till the visit of Borlase, the famous Cornish Antiquary, in the year
1752. He records, "the second church is in no
small danger." Even still this sanctuary slept on
—the subject only of tradition. A certain sand-
hill swelling higher than those around it, whereon
human bones were often found, was pointed to as
the place where the church of tradition was
buried. An old parishioner, Christopher Cotty
Jenkin, who has lived all his days in the neighbourhood of the sands, tells the writer he was the
first who saw any portion of the old church.
About fifty-five years ago he came to a spring in
the immediate neighbourhood to drink, and from
thence saw the "end of the church" just appear-
ing above the summit of the sand-hill. It was
an object of great interest, and no one doubted
but that it was the old church, which people used
to say had been buried there for centuries.

About thirty years afterwards, Gilbert, in his
Survey of Cornwall, states that the ruin then

visible consisted of two ends of a church, and several heaps of rubbish. Adjoining to these, on the south side, is the burial-ground, where there are scattered thousands of teeth and other human bones. Even whole skeletons lie exposed in regular order; and, strange as it may appear, the showers of sand that are continually wafted over this desolate spot scarcely ever alight on these melancholy relics of mortality. After this period several attempts were made by different persons to remove the sand from what has been termed its "passive victim." None, however, were successful till W. Michell, Esq., of Comprigney, with characteristic zeal and perseverance, accomplished in September, 1835, the work which had baffled so many before him. By his kind permission and obliging assistance, we are enabled to furnish an account of the state of this church when first restored. The hand of the spoiler has done much to injure it since, a period only of eight years. In a few years more it may be levelled with the sand, which has preserved it for so many centuries, and preserved it in sanctity and reverence, but which now protects it no longer.

Under Mr. Michell's directions the sand was thrown out with great difficulty from the interior by means of stages and platforms, and removed from all the exterior sides except the north. And thus was this little sanctuary, which had been for many centuries the object of tradition and deep

F

interest, once more restored from the darkness
and mystery in which it had been lost. There it
stood, the humble and unpretending monument
of the piety of simple times. Once more it
is restored to view; but with how different
feelings do we regard it now, compared with the
feelings of those who were compelled to forsake
their accustomed house of prayer !

How reluctantly those who had worshipped
within it forsook it,—with what pious care they
provided that, though buried and removed from
sight, it should still hold together to remotest
ages,—is evident from the state in which it was
found. The windows and doors had been built
up with stone to strengthen the walls ; the roof,
lest the weight of the sand should crush the
building, was carefully taken off and removed.
The chancel-rail, doors, and other fittings-up of the
church, were also taken away ; and it is due to the
character of the age to believe that all these
things were removed only to be appropriated again
to a similar sacred use in some other church, for
deeply they of old regarded the consecrated things
of God.

An examination of the locality in which the
church is discovered proves that it must originally
have been built in a little bay of the sea, or
" porth " (as it is termed in Cornwall); and that
this place, now occupied by wild and desolate
mountains of sand, was once a lowly valley, with its

little stream murmuring to the ocean—the same stream which for centuries restrained the sand from overwhelming the second church. The foundation of the church, like that of St. Levan in the west, near the Logan Rock, which is similarly situated in a valley opening to the sea, is laid in sand. The church lies nearly east and west, inclining only four degrees north of west.*

The external dimensions, taken when the sand was first removed, are as follows :—

Length . .	29 feet
Breadth . . .	16½
Height of gables .	19
Height of north and south walls	13
Thickness of the walls .	2

At that time, in the year 1835, it was in good preservation ; even the holes or steps in which the rafters rested, along the top of the side-walls, were as perfect as at that distant day when the rafters were taken out of them. The eastern wall,

* A question of orientation. St. Piran's day is the 5th of March ; at this period of the year the sun rises a few degrees south from east. If this church was not built on the principle of orientation,—that is, looking to that point where the sun rises on the festival of the patron saint,—it may still be —which is not improbable — that the disciples of St. Piran began to build soon after his death, and turned their church to that part of the heavens where the sun rose on the morning of laying the foundations ; which would have brought them very nearly indeed to the position in which we discovered the church.

which was pierced in two places, for a priest's door
and altar window, fell during the removal of the
sand.

The masonry of the walls, portions of which we
have endeavoured to represent faithfully in our
several illustrations, is of the rudest kind, and
cannot fail to strike the visitor as a strong evidence of the remote antiquity of the structure.
There is not any *lime* used in its construction, or
in the plastering of the interior of this building;
the substance employed in its stead is china-clay,
mixed with sand. The stones which form the
building are thrown together without any attempt
at regular courses, or any regard to what masons
term "joints." They consist of pieces of moor-
stone, quartz, porphyry, slate, &c., all collected in
the immediate neighbourhood; and some of them
round and smooth, as if taken from the bed of
a stream. All these appear to have been put
together in the rudest and simplest way, imbedded
in the clay-mortar, according to the Roman method, but without the tiles and flat stones the
Romans used, to bind their work. The largest
pieces of stone, particularly those which possessed an angle, seem to have been reserved for the
corners of the building, and for the sides of the
doors and windows. The masonry on the whole
looks like that of persons who had seen Roman
work, and perhaps assisted in it, without learning
the art; and who had seen lime and used it, but

without learning how it was prepared for use, and who pitched upon this white substance, china-clay, as resembling lime.

The principal entrance to this church was on the south side, nearer the west than the east end of the building. It was a small semicircular arched doorway, 7ft. 4in. by 2ft. 9in.; of parallel sides, *without splay.* The stone which forms the base of the doorway, which is raised about 2ft. 9in. from the ground, is much worn, as also the steps descending inward and outward, by the feet of the early Christians who worshipped at this oratory. We here give a representation of the doorway, copied from a rough sketch by W. Michell, Esq., at whose expense the church was cleared out. There is a moulding, it will be observed, round the door, in detail, unlike any which has hitherto been known in this country : and which, contrary to Norman and Saxon custom, is carried round the head of the arch, and down the sides of the doorway, without impost, or capital, and base. It is further ornamented with three heads; that of a leopard on the key-stone, and two human heads of different sizes, one on each side, at the spring of the arch. These ornaments are executed in elvan, a very soft stone found in the neighbouring cliffs. They are most rudely chiselled, or, we should say, merely scratched; for the features of the several faces, and the lines on the moulding, are roughly scratched with some rude instrument on the sur-

face of the soft stone. Simple and primitive as
these ornaments are, they were very possibly a
later insertion, for they were loosely fixed into the

DOORWAY OF THE OLD CHURCH.

outer angle of the doorway. This doorway was
in good preservation when first discovered, but
unfortunately was destroyed within a fortnight
after. Such was the interest it excited that,

stone by stone, the doorway began to disappear; whereupon it was deemed advisable to remove the three heads, the key-stone, and corbels, to some place of safety before they were stolen. They were afterwards deposited in the Museum in Truro, and with them one stone of the moulding, the only cut stone which could be found among the ruins in 1843, when the sand was again cleared out with very great difficulty, in order to make exact measurements of the church, and to rebuild the altar-tomb of St. Piran.

These four stones in the Museum are the only cut stones that remain of all those which formed this interesting doorway; the rest have been carried away as relics by selfish and destructive visitors, and cannot now be traced.

On the same side, about five feet from the southeast angle of the building, is a window—the rudest little window that was ever seen. We present a sketch of it, carefully taken, stone for stone. It is about five feet from the ground, and its dimensions are 1ft. 6in. by 1ft. Within the head of the archway there is a stone laid across to bear the weight of the wall above, although the radiating edges of the stones which form the semicircular head would appear as if they were upholding the ponderous weight. We leave our reader for the present to judge whether this is like a Norman arch, or a Saxon, or whether it looks more like a rude imitation of a Roman arch.

From this, let us pass on to the eastern side ;
the north and west walls are plain "dead walls,"
without any aperture.   In the centre of the east

EXTERIOR OF WINDOW OF THE OLD CHURCH.

wall, about five feet from the ground, there was
another window, but which, having been closed
up on the outside with stone, escaped notice till
last year.   In the northern corner of this wall
there was another round-headed doorway, somewhat smaller than the other, and without the ornaments ; but, like it, 2ft. 9in. from the ground, as-

cended by worn steps from the exterior as well as interior. The sides of this doorway are also parallel, and the angles sharp, without moulding or chamfer, possessing therefore another similarity to Roman structure. Through this doorway, which is probably the "priest's door," for the steps turn directly into the chancel, let us descend into the interior of this ancient sanctuary. The floor consists of a concrete, composed of a china-clay and coarse sand, and is hard and level. It is divided distinctly into chancel and nave,—the former 10ft., the latter 15ft.—making the internal length 25ft., its breadth being 12½ft. The chancel was separated from the nave by a rail or skreen, which

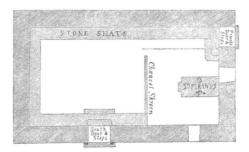

GROUND-PLAN.

must have been 5 or 6 feet high, as is evident by the groove in the south wall, and marks along the floor. These marks do not extend across the chancel, neither is there a corresponding groove

on the north wall; from which it is fair to infer
that the course of the skreen, and the limits of
the chancel, followed the dotted line we have
drawn in the ground-plan, running eastward to
the steps of the priest's door, leaving a passage
into the nave from the same entrance.   Another
reason for supposing this is, that the stone seats,
which on the south side stop at the chancel-rail,
are built round the nave along the remainder of
the south wall, along the west and the whole
length of the north, to the steps of the little door.
Another reason yet is, that the altar is placed, not
in the centre of the east wall, but in a centre
taken from the doorway, which we suppose was
the limit of the chancel.   Attached to the east
wall was an altar, built of stone, and plastered
like the rest of the interior.   In 1835 it was
taken down, and St. Piran's headless remains
were discovered immediately beneath it, as we
have described.

It has since been carefully rebuilt with the
same stones; a solid block of granite, nearly a
ton in weight, cut to the exact peculiar shape
and dimensions of the original altar, has been
placed over it; and as the altar is now, and
likely always to be, more a tomb than an altar, the
name of St. Piran has been deeply cut in the
granite, in early Roman characters.

This altar is peculiar in its position, as well as
its shape.   It lies lengthwise east and west, (not

north and south, as we now have them,) with
square pieces cut from the north and south angles
of the westernmost end of it.

This position and shape seem the most natural,
and just what we might expect an early altar-
tomb would be, which was designed by persons
who knew no peculiar rule or custom to follow.
There is the length to cover the body, which is
laid east and west ; the projecting piece to cover
the head. The dimensions of the altar are, as they
were :

	Ft.	In.
Length . . .	5	3
Breadth . . .	2	3
Height . . .	4	0

About ten inches above the altar, a little on
the north of it, and quite in the centre, equidistant
from the north and south walls, was a recess which
has since been cleared out, and proves to have been
a window, having a slight internal splay, plastered
within with china-clay. This window is two feet
wide, and was round-headed, and most probably
about two-and-a-half or three feet high. Its
arch, as well as that of the priest's door close by
it, have long since fallen in.

In the south wall of the chancel is the window
we have already noticed from the outside. The
interior view represents it as ruder than the exterior. In the latter there is a little architectural
display in the head of the arch ; but the masons

of other days could not afford to sacrifice any
more strength for effect, therefore the head of the
interior part of the window was differently devised, and plastered over with china-clay.   There
is a slight internal splay in this window also. The

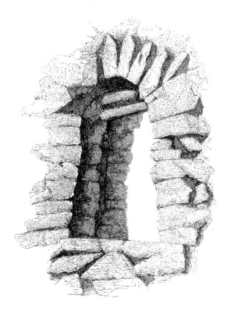

INTERIOR OF WINDOW OF THE OLD CHURCH.

stone seats which passed round the nave to the
priest's door are 1ft. 4in. high by 1ft. 2in. wide,
also plastered with china-clay.   There was no

wood found in this building except a small piece, eight inches long, two wide, and about one inch thick.

Such was this antient church in 1835, and almost so till 1838. In removing the sand from the south and east parts of the cemetery, another little structure was discovered by Mr. Michell, which we will describe in his own words, transcribed kindly from his memoranda respecting the Church of St. Piran in the Sands.

"15th Sept. 1835.

"About 100 yards from the church (south-east) are the ruins of a house now almost covered again with sand, which I explored. The dimensions of it were 16ft. by 12ft., and 10ft. high. The doorway, 7ft. by 2ft. 2in., was on the south side. The door had been removed; but its wooden door-case and threshold remained in their place, although in a very decayed state. This building had only one window, 12in. high by 6in. wide. The beams of this building I found in it nearly rotten. In the front of this house were thousands of mussel and limpet shells, together with fragments of earthen pots."

This little cell, which lies parallel with the church, is now almost buried in the sand again. The western gable end, and portions of the north and south walls, alone are visible: they are built in the same manner as the church, but of smaller stones, and are evidently of the same date as the church, or perhaps a little later ; for (the walls being built with smaller stones) the masonry does not look so clumsy, and there is, moreover, a slight attempt at "herring-bone" visible on the eastern side of the west gable.

The proportions of the church when entire must have been as peculiar as the structure of the walls, and equally rude. The narrow height of wall, not relieved by string-course or base-line, the scarcity of windows and their smallness, together with the raised threshold of the doorways, must have produced an effect unlike that of Norman and Saxon proportions ; but which, however correspond exactly with that of the ruins of the early churches in Ireland, many of which are attached to round towers, and evidently contemporaneous with them. Such was this church only a few years since. Its present state is deplorable and unchurchlike, and has induced many to pronounce that it is not, and never was a church ! — that it could not have been a church, for many reasons ! But, nevertheless, there are some few who are credulous enough to believe otherwise. At present the north and west walls alone are standing, for the most part entire ; the south and east, which were pierced for doors and windows, have long since become ruinous. Our frontispiece represents the present state of that portion of them which appears above the level of the sand,

and the little lake which is formed by the rising
of the water of the holy spring in the winter time.
Its " old enemy," the sand, which, however, preserved the sanctuary from more ruthless enemies
for many centuries, is gathering round it again, as
if jealous of its own dominion, and jealous of that
precious relic, now profaned and destroyed, which
for ages had shed such a charm and such deep
interest over the desolation and wild solitude of
its region.

CHAPTER III.

W<small>HAT</small> is the date of this oratory ? is a question
which is often asked, and often freely and confi-
dently answered, upon the authority of Mr. Bloxam. But, as we have said before, the structure
requires but to be seen, and its masonry, its shape,
and its dimensions to be but examined, to con-
vince the visitor that it cannot be Norman. Neither will it appear that it resembles in any respect
the Saxon remains which have hitherto been found
in Great Britain, or elsewhere. Such is the opinion the appearance of this oratory cannot fail to
suggest ; but it is a negative opinion ;—the question still remains, what is the date of this church ?
It is a question, too, which must be answered
under many difficulties and disadvantages ; not the
least among which is, the unbelieving character of
the age in which it is asked. It is untrodden
ground, and no one seems to have ventured upon
it. General prejudices are against believing that
a *stone structure* can be anterior to Saxon times.
Though too ready to believe what they would, and
what they desire to believe, men are not always
ready to believe all they may. They enter usually

upon judgment with a previously formed opinion : so it is with the comparatively trifling case before us ; so also, unfortunately, with great and important truths. Men too often believe what they will upon far less ground, than receive all they may upon greater.

We have shewn that Cornish antiquities are not subject to the rules and theories of architecture which are formed upon examples found in the central parts of England ; for this obvious reason, that the early history of those parts passes almost at one step from Roman to Saxon times ; while that of Cornwall, not to mention other parts, has an intermediate period of 500 years. The Saxons conquered the Britons in the central and more fertile parts of our island almost immediately after the departure of the Romans. They could not conquer the Cornish for 500 years after, till the year 930. It is to this intermediate period we have reason to refer the date of the structure in question. Every architectural evidence and every historical probability bear out our position ; while, on the other hand, there is nothing in the building peculiarly Saxon or Norman, but rather otherwise, and history and oral tradition equally afford no evidence whatever towards Saxon or Norman antiquity. Upon this ground we venture to ask for the oratory of St. Piran a British antiquity. We ask to refer it to the sixth century, and offer its masonry as a specimen of the imperfect and incipient style of building of the early British Christians, in Cornwall at least.

Here it may be permitted to observe, that the oratory of St. Piran is not the only structure of this period still remaining in Cornwall. There is another ancient church, at a place called *Gwithian*, about sixteen miles further west, upon the same coast, and preserved under exactly similar circumstances,—buried in sand. This church corresponds in general character with St. Piran's, and in masonry exactly. It has its cemetery and its well ; a doorway and small window on the south side, apparently the only apertures in this wall. It lies east and west; has a nave, chancel, and altar ; and in the north-east corner a priest's door, the base or threshold of which is also raised about two or three feet from the ground. In dimensions and internal arrangements, however, the church at Gwithian is somewhat different. The nave is 31ft. 6in. by 15ft. 5in. ; and in the east wall of the nave is a doorway 3ft. 7in. wide, which leads into a chancel, internally 14ft. 4in. by 12ft. 8in. There are no seats in the nave (probably they were of wood) ; but in the chancel there *are stone* seats, like those in St. Piran's, built in the same manner and about the same size. These are continued round the chancel to the altar, which is situated in the centre of the eastern wall. The altar is built of stone, and is about 4ft. 10in.

long from north to south, and probably was not more than 2ft. 6in. or 3ft. wide ; but it is in such a ruinous condition that it is impossible to ascertain its former dimensions. At present it is little more than 3ft. high, which is also the height of the walls of the chancel. The walls of the nave, in the highest parts, are about 8ft. high. The walls of this ruin are about 2½ft. thick, and are constructed in the same way as those of St. Piran's, with rough stones, of all shapes and sizes, put together without any *lime* in the mortar. This ruin is similarly situated, by the side of a stream on the sea-shore ; and for many centuries, with the land round it, had been overwhelmed in the same calcareous sand as at Perran-Zabuloe. It is little known, and unfrequented ; and the sacred dead rest in calm security beneath the rich green turf, which now covers the cemetery, and once covered the whole ruin. It was discovered about fifteen years ago by a neighbouring farmer, who employed his men to dig a pond in the vicinity of the spring or holy well.

In the course of excavation they came to many skeletons, and soon after to a portion of the eastern wall. Beneath this, under the altar, they found eight skeletons, ranged side by side, at a depth of three feet below the foundation.

Below these skeletons they struck upon the *ruins of another wall*, about three feet high, constructed rudely, like the upper wall. Beneath this again they found more skeletons, still in sand, at a depth of fifteen feet from the surface; here water hindered further search. They then proceeded to trace the walls all round, and to clear out the interior of the ruin.

The little window in the south wall was perfect, about two feet high and *round-headed*, but it soon after fell in. We have not yet been able to find any tradition or history of this church. St. Gwithian, who came over from Ireland a few years before St. Piran, was martyred by King Tewdor in this neighbourhood. Probably this structure was originally erected in honour and memory of the same holy martyr, to whom the present parish church, which lies within a quarter of a mile from the ruin, is dedicated, and the parish called after his name.* Like almost every other church in Corn-

---

* The name of this place in the Domesday Book of William the Conqueror is Conorton, or rather Canardi-tone. A manor of this name is still in existence. "There is a tradition," says the late Davies Gilbert, Esq., in his history of this parish, " supported by the authority of Leland, that a town, so large as to contain two churches, stood on this manor, which has been destroyed by sand ; but the tale must be, at least, a very great exaggeration." However this may be, in the sand, about a furlong from the ruin above described, *there is another cemetery*, and quantities of loose stone, which may have formed another church. These were discovered in cutting a new " *sanding* road" a few years ago. It would prove dangerous to remove the rich turf which now confines the sand, for the purpose of further investigation ; for

wall, this of St. Gwithian is also in the perpendicular style, and has a pinnacled tower, the proportions of which are beautiful, as also those of
the church itself; but unfortunately, like too
many Cornish churches, it is in wretched condition and repair—sadly symbolical of the spiritual
state of the Church in a country once so famous,
and deservedly renowned, for "loyalty to God and
the king." Besides the ancient ruin in Gwithian, there *is another* on the north coast of this
county, in the neighbourhood of Padstow. It is

nothing but that turf, humanly speaking, preserved the church
and church-town of Gwithian, from being utterly overwhelmed
with sand. In a sandy region, two miles westward from this
spot, a *buried village* has lately been traced by persons employed in carrying away sand for agricultural purposes. In the
course of a few months, when more of the sand is removed, it
will be practicable to examine this interesting place. At present there is not enough uncovered to give any opinion of the
date or character of the houses. Nothing at present is known
of this village, what was its name, or when it was overwhelmed. The following statement may give some idea of
the rapidity with which this light calcareous sand accumulates.
"The late Rector of the parish, the Rev. Mr. Hocken, stated to
Mr. Lyson that the barton of Upton, one of the principal
farms, was suddenly overwhelmed; that his great-grandfather
remembered the occupier residing in the farm-house, which
was nearly buried in one night! the family being obliged to
make their escape through the chamber windows; and that in
consequence of the wind producing a shifting of the sand. In
the winter of 1808-9, the house, after having been lost for
more than a century, again came to view." — *History of
Cornwall.*

situated in a portion of the parish of St. Minver,
which borders upon the sea near the little church
of St. Enodoc,* and probably was dedicated in
honour of the same saint. It was discovered
about fifty years ago in a high sand-hill ; and near
it there was a spring or holy well, and on the
south side a cemetery : but all traces of it are now
lost again.

In addition to these sanctuaries of the early
Christians of Cornwall which we have referred to,
there are ruins of others, and records of many
more, throughout the country, especially along the
coast. Some of these, it is true, bear traces of a

---

* This interesting church, in all probability, was originally
built when the above oratory was overwhelmed. It is situated near the huge sand-hill which contains the lost church,
but on the opposite side of a stream. It was probably erected
in this situation, like the second church of St. Piran, to be as
near the original sanctuary as possible, and in the hope that it
would be out of every danger of sharing the same fate. But,
unfortunately, subsequent eruptions of sand from the sea,
which is close by, within a quarter of a mile, have deluged the
opposite bank of the little river also ; and the chapel of St.
Enodoc is surrounded by sand-hills, which have risen as high as
the ridge of its roof. On first approaching this sacred edifice,
little can be discerned of it but its tiny tower, surmounted
with a crooked wind-worn spire of stone. The sand is now
in a manner subdued and kept down by grass, which has been
cultivated on its surface with diligent care and attention.
This is all which could have been done to save the church from
being entirely lost. The north side of it is, at this time, completely buried ; but on the east, south, and west sides the

comparatively late style of architecture; but in
many cases their names, their diminutive size,
and the vicinity of a spring and cemetery, indicate
that these small churches of Cornwall, though
rebuilt at a later date, were originally the oratories
of the early Cornish.

To return, then, to St. Piran's. We venture to
offer its masonry, its construction, its smallness,
and all its other peculiarities, as those of the early
architecture of the Celtic Christians. We say Celtic
Christians; for these peculiarities are by no means
confined to Cornwall, but are still to be found in

sand has been cleared away from the windows, to admit light
within; and in front of the porch a passage about eight or
nine feet deep has been cut, to afford admission to the church
for its regular though small congregation. This little church
was built about the year 1430, in the perpendicular style, and
is, with its sister church of St. Michael in the same parish,
very small in dimensions. It consists of a nave and chancel
under the same ridge of roof, a south transept, and eastward of
it a Lady chapel, beside the chancel. The tower is on the
north side, opposite the south transept. This church contains a
Norman font, which indicates the existence of a church *prior* to
the present structure; and another interesting indication of antiquity is in an ancient bell which once belonged to this church.
It was rudely cast, and bore the inscription " ALFREDVS
REX :" it was sold in the middle of the last century by the
churchwardens of the time, in order to defray the expenses of
repairs about the church. A portion of the old rood-screen,
which, according to Cornish custom, always extended across
the whole church, is still in existence, and a great portion of
the old carved open seats.

other places, which, like this county, remained
free from Saxon control and Saxon influence for
centuries after the central parts of the island,
—such, for instance, as Wales, and Anglesea, and
Guernsey, and Ireland, and, we believe, the same
peculiarities may be traced in Brittany also.
All these places afford evidences and examples
of a particular style, if we may use the term,
of ecclesiastical architecture which belonged to
the Celts, the original inhabitants of these islands
prior to the Saxon invasion. The writings of
our earliest historians confirm this opinion. The
oratory of St. Piran, therefore, we presume to be
British; and, if further confirmation be wanting,
it can be shewn that, *differing entirely* from
Saxon and Norman *remains*, it corresponds exactly with the sacred structures erected at this
period by the Irish, whose intimate connexion
with Cornwall so early as the fifth century we
have already had occasion to notice. The evidences we adduce will bring us to an early
period of the history of this county; that,
namely, which preceded its conquest by the
Saxons, and consequently that which immediately
succeeded the government of the Romans. Now
it will, perhaps, prove not a little interesting to
shew that St. Piran's corresponds *also* with the
churches which were built by the Christians early
in the fourth century during the reign of Constantine the Great, who, it will be remembered, was

the instrument, under God, to restore, or rather we should say, give peace and toleration to the early Christians both here and abroad. Hitherto they had suffered much from persecutions and oppression. Constantine the Great first openly tolerated Christianity, and, it is fair to believe, introduced into Britain the same customs which prevailed in other parts of his extensive dominions. It will, therefore, be not only interesting, but useful, to shew, first of all, the similarity of St. Piran's to the structures of the early Christians, *especially in the East*—at Byzantium and Antioch; which will also support us in our theory of the Eastern observances of the early British Church throughout Britain before the arrival of St. Augustine. In order, then, to trace the alleged similarity between St. Piran's and the early churches of the fourth century, let us briefly inquire into the character of the latter.

We find, then, that as soon as the decree of Constantine the Great openly sanctioned and acknowledged Christianity, the early Christians seem, one and all, in all parts of the very extensive empire under Constantine's sole government, to have not only set to the pious work of erecting churches with zeal and alacrity, but to have followed simultaneously one and the same form and arrangement in their structures. That form and arrangement, under these circumstances, we may presume had been agreed upon and handed down from former generations. Of these, it should

be premised, that they prove upon examination to
be a comprehensive and significant form and arrangement, not adopted for convenience, but with a
deeper and a holier aim—that of expression and
symbolism. This is the character of the ecclesiastical architecture of the early Christians.
They seem to have intended, by the material
fabric, to figure the spiritual edifice, and thus to
lead the mind of the devout Christian, previous to
his entering upon the sacred duties for which it
was set apart, from the earthly to the heavenly
Jerusalem, of which the former was intended
to be the type. This is no fanciful opinion : all
churches, more or less, have been built upon
this significant plan, from the earliest times to
the present; and the writings of the early Fathers
allude to these forms, and decorations, and arrangements as symbolical : they write of them as
intentionally so, as if their meaning were defined
and fully understood. Nor is it at all improbable
that this should have been the case, when we consider through whom the Gospel has been transmitted to us. Salvation has been to us, in more senses
than one, from the Jews : the Jewish race gave birth
to the Messiah—the Jews have handed to us the
Moral Law of God—the Jews were the first apostles, and for the most part the first teachers of the
Gospel of the New Covenant—to them, humanly
speaking, we are indebted for the truths of the
Gospel—they have proved, for the most part, the

channel through which the glad tidings of the
Gospel have come to us, although, under God's
inscrutable dispensation, they themselves now
remain ignorant of its tidings. Their religion
was symbolical and highly mystical. In it, in
its ordinances of worship, and in its Temple, were
shadowed from the beginning, we may say pro-
phetically, the great mysteries of the latter Dispensation. Their Temple, especially the great
Temple of Unity,—for thither all true Israelites
assembled to worship with one accord, — that
Temple was symbolical throughout in its form
and arrangements. Built under the commands
of the Most High God, the several parts and
decorations even, of the Temple had each and
all their comprehensive, dark, and mysterious,
and prophetic meaning. We find St. Paul, in his
Epistle to the Hebrews, affectionately endeavouring
to confirm the faith of his converted countrymen
by this very subject of symbolism : he opens to
them the dark, mysterious meaning of the various
parts of their late religion and the Temple, and
explains their fulfilment in the new Dispensation.
It is probable, therefore, that these Hebrew
Christians in their subsequent designs of churches
studied to follow a system which custom and
habit had long endeared, and which had proved so
interesting and significant. Therefore to them,
our earliest brethren, we are indebted for the
symbolical character of our ecclesiastical archi-

tecture. This art, preserved through three centuries of dire persecutions, we see, when persecutions were at an end, universally and simultaneously followed, and especially by the Emperor
Constantine the Great. How interesting is it to
trace, in our earliest remains and records, similarity to the several peculiarities of this style!
We may fairly affirm it was introduced to this
country in the time of the great Emperor. Still
to this day the holy symbolic art remains in this
our favoured land!—in its purity it remains, though
marred often by superstition on the one hand,
and hard unbelief on the other : it still continues
in spirit and in character, speaking the same
pure language it spoke long centuries ago.

From the writings of the fourth century we learn,
first, that a portion of land was enclosed,* separated

* It is not known when this enclosed space was first used
for the purpose of burial. We learn from Bingham, that,
among the primitive Christians, burying in *cities* was not allowed for the first three centuries, nor in "*churches strictly so
called*" for many years after. The earliest canon we have been
able to find on this subject is one of the Council of Nantes,
which was held in the year 658. This canon allows *general
burial* in porches and out-buildings of the church. The pro-
hibitions above given as to burials, only refer to cities,
churches, and out-buildings of the latter, and not to the precincts of a church. We shall see presently that at a very
early period churches were erected over the remains of apostles, and martyrs, and confessors. The same pious feelings
which induced the early Christians to do this, would have
led them to deposit the remains of others, whom they rever-

from the world, as it were, and all secular purposes, and consecrated to the service of God. It contained within its limits, and generally upon its boundary, a spring of water for the appointed cleansing. This we find the indispensable accompaniment of a central early church, intentionally

enced, near the church, if not within it ; and thus at an early period the custom of burying in the enclosed space round the church may have been fully established. Gregory the Great, about the end of the seventh century, writes in favour and approbation of the custom of burying near a church : he sanctioned and encouraged it. As when on earth Christians turned to the east in prayer and devotion, so, when they exchanged this state of existence for another, they were deposited looking upward and eastward, as if for the coming of the Lord. There is a tradition that bishops and priests were buried with face to the west, as they stood in ministering to their respective flocks, who were looking eastward ; and that they will come with the great Judge hereafter, to call those who had been entrusted to their care, to judgment. No passage or inference in Holy Scripture, however, can sanction the reason assigned for this different position of burial for the ministry. We are all indiscriminately, all and every one, commanded to await and watch the dread advent of the Judge. There are only a few examples of this to be found in England ; one, we understand, in the church at Clovelly, in North Devon.

We may be permitted here to notice the custom of carrying the dead with psalmody to the grave ; it is still observed in Cornwall, and was the usage of the East so early as the fourth century. Thus St. Chrysostom writes on the subject : " What mean our hymns ? do we not glorify God and give Him thanks that He hath crowned him that is departed—that He hath delivered him from trouble—hath set him free from all fear ? Consider what thou singest at that time."

symbolical of the necessity of baptism ; for, however we may neglect this holy sacrament now,
it was not neglected then, and in serious reality
must not be neglected. Its necessity is not nul-
lified by an opinion ; it is decreed in words which
cannot pass away, that without it no one shall enter
the kingdom of God; S. John iii. 5—7. With the
element of water it has been promised the rege-
nerating influence will descend, and seal once and
for eternity, whether effectually or otherwise, the
children of God and inheritors of the kingdom of
heaven. In those days, a spot of land so furnished with a spring was not denied. Devotion
to God was the first consideration of the period ;
it swayed more than all other considerations ;
and Nature, the faithful handmaid of God, as if to
emulate the pious devotion, seems in almost all
cases to bestow beauty around a spring and well ;
and thus in a beautiful and retired locality,
appropriate for the position of a church, the little
structure reared its simple head. A peculiarity
of the time, which deserves particular notice,
is, that the baptistery was distinct from the
church, never in it, and seldom even touching it.
Eusebius, in the fourth century, speaking of the
church which Paulinus built at Tyre, says, when
that curious artist had finished his famous structure within, he then set himself about the exedræ
or out-buildings, by which places he tells us he
chiefly meant the place which was for the use of

those who " needed cleansing and sprinkling of
water, and the Holy Spirit." Constantine, we
learn, built churches at Antioch and elsewhere
which were furnished with the usual exedræ ;
and again, Paulinus, Bishop of Nola, says, in his
Epistle to Severus, that he had built two churches
with a baptistery between them. St. Austin also
intimates that the baptistery was distinct and apart
from the church, and that there were separate
apartments in it for the men and women likewise ;
which, perhaps, may be the reason why St. Ambrose speaks of it in the plural number, thus,
" the baptisteries of the church."—Bingham, book
viii. ch. 7. Besides the baptistery, there were
other out-buildings set apart for religious purposes within the limits of the consecrated precincts. One of these we will especially notice,
which was the most general and most constant
companion of the baptistery. It is called, in the
Apostolical Canons, pastaphorium, and corresponds
with our word " cell." This place was used for
keeping the consecrated vessels of the church, and
the elements of bread and wine for the Lord's
Supper, and the alms of the people. And also,
says Bingham, it was a habitation for the bishop
or clergyman, or the guardian and keeper of the
church, as Schelstrate rightly concludes from a
passage in St. Jerome, where he explains pastaphorium to be the chamber or habitation where
the ruler of the Temple dwelt. These two were

the most important and most usual accompaniments of every church. From the baptistery a path, symbolical of the efficacy of the baptismal rite, led to the church ; but, before we enter, let us examine its position. It lies east and west universally. We are accustomed to see churches built in this position; to us it is nothing strange : but, if it has no meaning, is it not stranger still that many churches should have been built at the same time, and in different countries, and all pointing to the east ? But there is a meaning in it which must place beyond doubt that the position was intentional and premeditated. The Jews in the old Dispensation, in their devotions, turned towards Jerusalem, the holy city, which was the type of the light of the Gospel. In the present and new Dispensation, our Lord is to us our light ; the sun which rises daily is His symbol to us, and should ever remind us of Him, and of His future coming. Our duty, as His servants, is to be ever looking for that light, His second advent ; as the Jews looked, and blindly still look, for His first. We should do this in compliance with His affectionate request to " watch and pray," and also in obedience to His positive command ever to be mindful of His coming. We turn, then, eastward in expectancy ; thus have all Christians in all ages and countries done, and their churches have indicated and still indicate the same obedient watchfulness. There was always a window in the east wall over the altar as if to carry out the idea of this symbolical watching more completely. In reverence to the memory of Saint or holy Martyr, in the cause of the Church, Christians from early times have turned, it is supposed, to the point of the horizon where the sun appears on the festival of the tutelary Saint to be commemorated : that point was regarded the east, the symbolical east of that day. Hence the slight variations which are seen in the position of our churches at this day. Or, if this opinion will not be received, and cannot be established, we may suppose,—for some reason there must be for the variations alluded to, — we may suppose the builders turned to the sun rising on the day of laying the foundation, considering that position the true east, but still in compliance with some significant custom.

Let us come now to the doorway of the early churches. We find a path from the baptistery leading directly to the principal entrance, which is always found at or near the west end of the edifice, indicative of the state of pupilage and discipline which it is appointed should lead to perfect devotion. Here the newly-admitted servant of God entered from the baptistery, through a low portal, bowing in humility, into the House of God. It is the House of the Lord ; here the world and worldly thoughts are banished from the mind. The interior of the church was symbolical

H

of that entire devotion which God requires from
His servants ; entire and exclusive devotion, " for
we cannot serve two masters." Every church was
distinctly divided into chancel and nave, which
was indicative of the twofold character of human
devotion ; namely, that which is required from
men called to be the ministers of God to their
fellow-men, and secondly, that which is required
from those who are ministered to. The nave is
for the latter, wherein were the appointed places
of those who held offices of secular authority,—
four divisions, for four states of life : here a place
for the married—there for the unmarried ; here
for the men, generally the north side,—and there
for the women. All had their own places symbolical of their own respective duties.

Through the nave a passage led to the chancel,
but an impassable rail of division indicated here
the real and positive distinction between chancel
and nave ; that is, between the appointed ministers of God and the people. This rail we find as
customary as its meaning renders it necessary.
Eusebius, describing a chancel, (a word of Latin
derivation, from *cancelli*, rails,) says the altar
was divided from the rest of the church by
certain rails of wood curiously and skilfully
wrought in the form of net-work, to make it *in-
accessible* to the multitude. Theodoret also, writing on the same subject, uses the usual Greek
phrase which corresponds with our word chancel,

" the space within the *rails ;*" which, it will be
observed, is equally decisive : and Synesius also
affords evidence in his phrase, "*to lay hold of the
rails ;*" meaning thereby to take sanctuary or re-
fuge.   The rail, then, we see, was never omitted
in early times, neither was the marked distinction disregarded between the minister of God and
the people.   As the nave, in its distribution, was
indicative of the duties of the people, so the
chancel also was furnished equally in reference to
its own meaning, and was symbolical of the duties
of the clergy.   First, it contained the altar—the
one altar symbolical of the one great Sacrifice—
where the priest " waited," and from thence
ministered to his people.   It contained also three
graduating seats for the three orders of the appointed ministry.   Within this space the ministers of God were enclosed by an impassable rail
of division, distinct from the people, and set apart
to do the work of God for the good of men.
Hither God has appointed the faithful should
look for the means of grace and pardon and
reconciliation.   The position of the chancel was
symbolical to this end, lying between the people
and the east, where was the object of their devotion.   The ministers of God wait in that intermediate space, and administer to the spiritual wants
of the people ; to intercede on their behalf, not in-
tercept, but forward their petitions to the Throne
of Grace.

The altar, then, whereon it has pleased the Lord to place " His Holy Name there," was intentionally placed in the east. Before the time of Constantine the Great, altars were generally formed of wood ; we learn from St. Austin, who lived in the third century, that they were of wood in the African Church in his time ; Optatus also implies that altars were of wood. Athanasius writes thus on the subject : " Communion-tables were of wood, as also the throne and seat of the presbyters." But after the conversion of Constantine, about the year 320, altars began to be constructed *of stone*. Constantine erected several altars of stone, and in some of his more splendid churches they were "covered over *with silver*." Gregory Nyssen, writing soon after this period, in his discourse on Baptism alludes thus to the stone subject : " This altar," says he, " whereat we stand, is by nature only *common stone*, whereof *our walls are made ;* but, after it is consecrated to God, it becomes a holy table, an immaculate altar, which may not be promiscuously touched by all, but only by the priest in time of divine service."

Here we have given a description of the position and arrangement of the churches of the early Christians of the fourth century. Thus beautifully and harmoniously, full 1500 years ago, were the several parts of the sanctuary arranged ; it was the studied, intentional plan of our earliest brethren—ages and generations have confirmed the wisdom of it—and, with only a few alterations, it should be our pride to remember that the same symbolical plan is with us to this day. The inclemency of climate has driven the principal entrance of the church to the south, though there are very few churches indeed which have not a western doorway also ; and for the same reason, probably, the Saxons introduced the font within the church ; but in both these cases the spirit, if not the letter, of the significant plan has been preserved. The south entrance is placed near the west end of the church, as also the font, near to it. Thus is our ecclesiastical architecture symbolical, and, we may add, worthily so. It is worthy that an art, which is, as it were, dedicated to the service of God, should have more than the mere beauty of its proportions, or the value of its ornaments, to recommend it to our attention. How much more worthy is it of such structures that they should not only gratify the eye with their beauty and elegance, and the heart with reverence for the piety of those who built them, but also that that beauty and elegance and piety should all unite in speaking to the faithful a mystical language, and remind them of their spiritual state, as it is, and it will be ! Yes : the ancient and significant, and it is our glory to add the national, architecture of our Church has a language ; as if God Himself had given to inanimate structures a voice to speak, since the

time that the Lord directed Solomon to build His
symbolical Temple at Jerusalem. Strangely it
speaks, even when the pious efforts of human ingenuity never intended it to speak. The opinions and doctrines and even tones of thinking
in each succeeding age from the beginning seem
to have taken substantial form, and to speak
to us at this distant day, the mystic chroni-
cle of the faithful! Strangely it speaks of simplicity and the purity of ancient faith, of advancing skill and advancing piety and devotion; but
it is too much to expect a long continuance of the
same lofty strain. Man is prone to fall: while
persecutions and troubles were at hand, religion
was zeal and firm attachment, and while the
heart still glowed with gratitude for deliverance
from bitter trials; but too soon in prosperity did
man's heart seek out many inventions. Ecclesiastical architecture tells the sad tale of declining
purity and rising superstition—of rising love of
the world, and pomp, and display of empty vanity.
In ruin and spoliation, it tells of fanaticism, and
worse than Pharisaical sanctity. Thus may we
trace the history of our Church in its architecture,
from right to wrong, from wrong to over-right;
trace its past state, and compare it with the present. Strange language! how often does it tell
of piety and devotion, and often again of cold
neglect. There is not a church in all the land
which has not its simple tale. Too often, in neg-

lect and dilapidation, it mournfully tells how love has grown cold, and piety departed. Still it stands open, and ready to receive its children still, the few who have not turned away. Once the pride and glory of her children, many, many a church feebly calls, and often calls in vain ; and even in ruin warns the heedless of the consequences of neglect. But, thanks be to God ! our country seems to be rising from her long lethargy. There are many churches throughout the land which speak more joyfully in these days ; which tell of acts of piety and acts of self-denial, done often in secret, for the honour of God and His Church. These have a voice too ; their language is of thankfulness : they sing the song of praise to the wakeful faithful heart in the still night, when the world is, as it were, lost in sleep ; these sing on in the silence the praises of our God ; they tell of grace and blessing descending upon our beloved land ; they tell of returning piety and zeal, of returning love and self-denying devotion ; devotion which seeks not the praise of men, but does all for the glory and honour of God. Many, many churches restored to their original beauty and order, and many others which have risen and are rising around us, speak in the voice of hope, and assure us that the mighty stream of zeal and piety now flowing so irresistibly, is not in vain ; it flows in cause of the Most High God and His holy Church ; it is strong,

therefore, and will flow on, and tell to generations
yet to come how God has continued to bless our
land.   It will be a blessing, and be blessed ; it
has the Almighty's unfailing promise ; the Lord
will not forsake His people.   He will never
forsake His Church, " for His great name sake, because it hath pleased Him to make us His people."

To return, then, to our immediate subject, the
churches of the fourth century.   We have shewn
the form and internal arrangement of them at
this early period of the history of the Church ;
let us pass on to another custom with regard
to them which is worthy of notice.   We find
they were often erected *over the burial-places* of
saints and martyrs, who were esteemed and
reverenced for piety or suffering, or both.   During
the period of which we are treating this was a
common custom ; particularly at this time, when
the late persecutions and trials under Diocletian
had endeared the memory of those who had
suffered and gone to their rest.   It is one of the
blessings of affliction that it draws nearer to us
in person and attachment those who have been
involved in it with ourselves.   It was a natural
though a melancholy desire in the survivors of
the troubles of the second century to cherish
the memory of those whom they reverenced, and
perhaps reverenced the more since they had been
removed from them.   It was a holy and godly
and a happy sorrow which sought consolation in

bereavement by associating the memory of the
departed with the duties of worship and praise
to that God who had inflicted that sorrow!
Still, even at that time there were some to cavil,
and to object to this act of worship to God
associated with homage to man! We find St.
Austin thus firmly defending the pious custom, and at the same time explaining it. " We
build not temples to our martyrs as gods, but
only memorials of them as dead men whose spirits
live with God; nor do we erect altars to them
in those memorials, or offer sacrifice thereon to
our martyrs, but to the only God, both theirs and
ours." In times of persecution the early Christians were accustomed to meet in the private
vaults and burying-places, and especially at the
graves of martyrs. The canons of the Council
of Eliberis, which was held in the heat of the
Diocletian persecution, several times allude to
the congregations which assembled at such places,
and we find the edicts of persecuting emperors
publicly prohibiting such wonted assemblies.
However these commands were obeyed at the
time, the feelings of reverence survived till after
the persecution, when the Christians proceeded to
erect oratories over those graves of martyrs and
others which they had been forbidden to frequent
before. Hence the term " cœmeteria," which is
sometimes applied to the early churches, and the
term "martyrium," which we had occasion to allude

to before ; and those of " apostoleum" and "propheteum," which are also used at this period.
Sozomen writes of the apostoleum of St. Peter
at Rome, and the apostoleum of St. Paul and
St. Peter near Chalcedon ; and elsewhere we find
mention of the " propheteum of Esaias," and that
of " Samuel, in which his relics were laid up."
All these terms were in common use, and generally understood to denote churches erected over
the burial-place and in memory of martyrs and
apostles and prophets. In allusion to this custom of building over the graves of holy men,
St. Chrysostom writes, " One might see *whole
cities* running to the monuments of martyrs ;"
and again, " We depart not from their sepulchres ; here kings lay aside their crowns, and
continue praying for deliverance from dangers,
and for victory over their enemies." Nay, he
triumphs that the " apostles in their death were
more honourable than the greatest kings upon
earth ; for even at Rome, the royal city, emperors
and consuls and generals left all, and ran to the
sepulchres of the fisherman and tent-maker ; and
at Constantinople it was thought honour enough
by those that wore the diadem to be buried, not
with the apostles, but before their porches, and
kings themselves became the door-keepers of fish-
ermen !" Thus " mightily grew the word of the
Lord and prevailed !" But a century before, and
the servants of God were the outcasts and the

despised of the people ; now kings did homage to them ! This custom of building oratories over the graves of martyrs and others, and especially in cemeteries, probably led eventually to the peculiarly Christian usage of burying the departed near the place of worship. The tone and character of these early times justify us in supposing that our primitive brethren were equally capable with us of appreciating a custom so appropriate to our hopes, and in other respects so worthy to be observed. The heathen, who had no certain hope beyond the grave, thought not to associate their dead with their religious devotions ; they deposited them in outskirts of their cities, and in unfrequented places ; but with the Christian the case is far different. No place can be so appropriate for his resting-place as the frequented precincts of that church in which he has worshipped, and where his hopes of eternity have been formed and advanced. To lie down to his rest when his toil is done, among his brethren who have gone before him, and beneath the shadow of the venerable church of his fathers, is truly and appropriately a Christian's hope. It is an appropriate custom also with respect to the feelings and the consolations of survivors ; our hearts naturally yearn towards those who have been taken from us : to what place more appropriately could our thoughts be carried than to the hallowed precincts where the dead rest in peace — the

sacred precincts of the Church of God, which
ever should be a source of consolation and our re-
fuge in trouble?—and deep and lasting consolation
has it afforded to many, and will afford still to
all who will seek it there. How superficial then
is the excuse which is often urged for non-attend-
ance at the services of the Church, that the
mourner cannot bear to frequent the House of
God so frequently as he was wont ! The Christian should not fear to be reminded of sorrow
and death, and most especially in that holy place
where there are stores of comfort and balm to
soothe his pain and to heal his wounds. Our
primitive brethren were not incapable of such
feelings as these. Once suggested to them, as it
most probably was by the circumstances above
alluded to, we cannot suppose they deferred long
before they adopted a custom so congenial to
Christian hopes and Christian consolation.

In each and all these points which we have
been considering, and especially in those which,
compared with existing customs, are distinctive
and peculiar to the early Christians, we find the
oratory of St. Piran accords with the churches
of the fourth century. It is erected over the
burial-place of St. Piran, a bishop and a confessor ; it lies east and west, with a slight inclina-
tion to that point of the horizon where the sun
appears on or about the 5th of March, which is
St. Piran's day. It has its principal entrance

near the west ; it is internally divided into chancel and nave, and possesses to this day the marks of the rail which divided them. It has a stone altar, and a small window above it looking eastward. It is surrounded by consecrated precincts, which are enclosed by a wall, portions of which have been seen at different times when the wind has disturbed the sand. It has an out-building, which accords with the descriptions of the ancient pastaphorium, and evidently was intended for the same purpose ; and lastly, it has a spring within twenty yards of it, in an easterly direction, towards the amphitheatre we have referred to, and the probable site of the dwellings of the original inhabitants of this district. Here we may imagine was the entrance to the enclosed space in which the church was built, where the baptistery stood, and perhaps stands to this day beneath the sand.

Thus far we trace a similarity between this structure and the structures of early Christians abroad ; and let it be humbly submitted, the similarity we have traced is not a fanciful but a serious one, and one of importance to our subject. The period of which we have been treating is the great epoch in the history of the Church. In this century not only did persecution cease, but the holy religion of peace was openly acknowledged, and, by God's blessing, adopted as the religion of the first empire in the world ; kings and emperors after this become its " nurs-

ing fathers," and queens its " nursing mothers."
Under the protection of Constantine the Great,
the forms and ceremonies of religion began to be
developed throughout all the Roman empire, not
excepting Britain. Let it be remembered also
that the writers we have referred to are those
who give us the history of the Church in the
neighbourhood of Constantinople and other places,
where, afterwards, when the schism between the
Eastern and Western branches of the Church
began, the custom called Eastern or Greek, from
the former branch, were maintained and defended.
By the glimmering light of our early history we
find that the same custom prevailed in this country also among its original inhabitants. This
circumstance will prove an additional argument
in favour of the similarity we have traced between this oratory and the oratories of the
churches abroad.

It is but reasonable to suppose that the Romans introduced the same customs to this country
which they observed abroad, especially in Constantinople the capital of their empire ; and reasonable also to suppose that the British, after
the final departure of the Romans, in retaining
the religion, retained also the customs which they
had in a great measure received from their former
masters, and observed together with them. To
this, then, we have attributed the similarity which
we have traced between the churches of the fourth

century and the oratory of St. Piran ; and, if our premises are not unreasonable, we may venture yet farther, and suppose that all the early churches erected in this country by the Roman British, and by the British after the departure of the Romans, also corresponded with the same models which we find in the writings of the early Fathers and historians of the Church ; and therefore we may presume to state that St. Piran's was not a solitary instance of similarity to those primitive structures, but one of many others, which, under peculiar circumstances, has been preserved to this distant day. There is then a reasonable probability in supposing that we may regard St. Piran's oratory as a fair specimen of the structures of the British times. We have so few records of those times, and so few remains, that it is difficult to make any positive statement. We are compelled to follow conjectures and probabilities. But thus much we may say in favour of our conjecture, that all the few records we can gather, directly or indirectly, and all the remains which are still in existence, bear out the alleged correspondence between St. Piran and the structures of those early times ; and, what is more, these not only agree among themselves, but in some *important points* differ from Saxon remains, and more so yet from Norman.

We learn from Gildas, our earliest historian, that the Diocletian persecution raged very severely in

Britain, and that many churches were destroyed ; but that, after the persecution had ceased, the Romans and British built their churches again new from the ground, and many more besides, as so many trophies of their martyrs. Here, then, at the very onset, so early as the beginning of the fourth century, we find the Christians in Britain following exactly the same custom with respect to the position and dedication of their churches as that we have noticed above. After this, records fail us ; and again, after a few centuries, by the faint light of early history we find that other customs, similar to those observed in the East, were still remaining among our countrymen. As time advances and the light of history becomes brighter, we see the British, even through persecution, and troubles, and ejectment from portions of their own country, still observing the same, and with jealous tenacity defending them to the last, while their liberty remained.

In the mean time, during the course of these centuries of persecution, in secure and remote places churches are built, what is the character of them ? We have no minute descriptions of them, but the earliest writers whose works have reached our time give us a general impression of their character. They had means of ascertaining this which we have not, and it is interesting in this general character to trace the exact peculiarities of St.Piran's.

But, before we come to the evidence we derive from our historians, there is yet another source of information on this point, which we think is not to be despised ; we refer to our old writers ; they give no architectural description, but some valuable information nevertheless. Spenser, for instance, who was deeply read in the early chronicles and legends of the British and Irish of early times, gives us some general impression on the subject, many of which are out of our reach now. The general character of religious edifices he mentions in the course of the Faerie Queene and other works is, that they are small " and lowly chappels," beside their gushing springs, and the little hermitage. Again, in a curious old work entitled the " Byrth, Lyf, and Actes of Kinge Arthure," first printed by Caxton in 1485, there are similar allusions to the character of the sacred edifices of early times ; at chapter xvii. we have the following : " And at the last Sir Lancelot came to a stony crosse, whiche departed two wayes in waste lande ; and by the crosse was a stone that was of marbel, but it was so derke that Sir Lancelot myghte not wete what it was. Thenne Sir Lancelot, he loked by hym and saw an old *chappel*, and ther he wend to have fonde peple." And elsewhere in this work we have mention of " holy chappels and fayr aulters, full rychely arrayed with clothe of clene sylke, whereon stode fayre candlestyks whiche were of silver ;" and " the

spring al silverie, and the hermitage and crosse."
These we urge not as authority, but they may
still be received for the purpose we have quoted
them,—to afford a general impression of the character of early churches. Some doubt that such
a person as the renowned King Arthur ever lived,
but that is not the point ; we have not to do
with the subject-matter of the work, but with
its casual and undesigned allusions to certain
features of scenery, let us call them. We have
reason, too, to believe that these chapels and
crosses are not merely imaginary but taken from
real existing chapels and crosses of the time to
which they refer ; for to this day, in the places and
among the people that the renowned Sir Lancelot
" is said to have rod in quest of the Sancgrael,"
there are remains of lowly chapels, and crosses,
and springs, and hermitages. However, let us
not be supposed to be trifling with the credulity
of our readers ; we have graver testimony to adduce in favour of this character of the early
churches among the Celts. To this day, we have
said, there are remains of small churches, and
crosses, and holy wells, and " hermitages :" they
are to be found in places where the original inhabitants of these islands remained comparatively
free, such as Cornwall, and Wales, and Ireland, and
Guernsey, and Anglesea ; these places we have had
occasion to refer to before. St. Piran's will bear to
be compared with these, and to be classed with them.

But there is other evidence which we gather from the allusions of our early historians. We, who are accustomed to larger churches, and many windows and a font within the church, are struck as we contemplate St. Piran, with its peculiarities under these heads : first, its smallness, and paucity of windows ; secondly, its want of a font within. We find some of our earlier historians have selected these very points as worthy of notice ; very probably for the same reason that we notice them, their peculiarity in these respects. Let us take first its smallness : this we suppose to be an evidence of the remote antiquity of this structure, and to be peculiar to early times.

The earliest churches in these islands appear generally to have been *small*. Bingham attributes this to the poverty and uncertainty attendant on times of persecution. Mathew of Paris, in describing the Church or Martyry erected by the British over their first martyr, St. Alban, uses the word " Ecclesiola"—small church : he writes at a period when churches were usually built larger ; and hence, probably, his especial notice of the smallness of St. Alban's. William of Malmesbury also uses the same word frequently in his accounts of the early churches of the British. From Venerable Bede, too, we obtain some little evidence. In his general descriptions he does not enter upon the subject of size ; he calls them oratories, and we may infer that they were

of the customary size of the time. But, in describing the church Bishop Paulinus built at Lin-
coln, he calls it a large church, as if it were an
exception to the usual structures ; and we have
some reason for supposing it was, for St. Nynyan's
in Scotland, which he mentions, as others, without
reference to size, proves to have been *very small.*

We come now to the second peculiarity we
have to notice,—the Baptistery distinct from the
Church. There is no font in St. Piran's, nor
even traces on the concrete floor to mark where
one stood ; therefore we have concluded that the
spring in the immediate neighbourhood was the
baptismal well belonging to the oratory. In this
respect it can be shewn that St. Piran's corresponds with the early British custom ; and not only
so, but it *differs from that of the Saxons.* We
will confine ourselves to the testimony of Venerable Bede for this matter, and begin with his account of the Saxon usage with regard to the Sacrament of Baptism. We gather from his history that in his time and among his countrymen
it was customary to baptize "within" the oratory.
The following is his account of the erection of
an early, if not the first, Saxon church in England : " On Easter-day, April 12, 627, Edwyn
king of Northumbria was baptized at York *in*
the church of St. Peter, which he himself built
of timber, 'while he was catechising and instruct-
ing, in order to receive baptism.' * * *   But, as

soon as he was baptized, he took care, under the
directions of Paulinus, whom he made Bishop of
York, to build a *larger* and *nobler church of stone,*
in the midst whereof that same oratory was enclosed." "Parts of this fabric," says the Rev.
Ayliffe Poole,* " were discovered beneath the choir
of the present cathedral during the repairs ren-
dered necessary by the mad act of the incendiary
Jonathan Martin. In the first number of Brown's
History of the Edifice of the Metropolitan Church
of St. Peter, York, in plate iii. is given a plan
of Paulinus' second edifice ; where the probable
position of the wooden baptistery, *enclosing a
spring still remaining,* is pointed out, and, though
obscured by several successive subsequent erec-
tions, this discovery is very valuable to the Ecclesiastical antiquary."

This interesting discovery explains beyond a
doubt the Saxon historian's meaning, of persons
being *baptized* IN *oratories.* He writes thus more
than once, implying that it was the universal
custom in his time among the Saxons.† But we
find an important exception to this custom.
There was a *spring beside* the stone church of
St. Nynyan in Scotland : this worthy bishop, he
informs us, came from Ireland, and observed

* Lectures on the Structure and Decorations of Churches.
† The font in St. Martin's church at Canterbury is supposed to be Saxon, and to have been fixed in its present position by the Saxons.

Easter according to the custom of the Greek
Church.

And again, he thus describes St. Cuthbert's
oratory at Lindisfarne. The holy bishop "built
a small house and made a trench about it. He
then commanded his brethren to dig a pit in the
floor, although the ground was hard and stony,
and no hopes appeared of a spring. Having done
this, *upon faith*, and at the prayer of the servant
of God, the next day it appeared *full of water*,
and to this day affords plenty of its heavenly
bounty to those that resort thither. * * Beside
this fountain he built an oratory."

The spring which afforded the heavenly bounty
in this case is not within the house of prayer,
and there is a reason for it. St. Cuthbert was a
bishop from Ireland, and, though living among
Saxons, he still retained to the last the customs
of the Eastern Church.* Hence we learn what
was the British and Irish observance with regard
to the Sacrament of Baptism, and also that the
Saxons were the first in England to introduce
the font within the church ; a custom which the
Normans followed, and all succeeding generations
have continued to observe.

* When his grave and coffin, in Durham Cathedral, were
opened for the purpose of gratifying curiosity in 1827, a small
Greek cross was discovered on his breast, which was *taken out*,
and is now to be seen in the Library of the Dean and Chapter,
together with an ivory comb and portions of his embroidered
vestments, which were entire.

The oldest fonts which remain to the present
time are Saxon, and they are found in those parts
of England where the Saxons became naturalized,
and there alone; we have not been able to find
any traces of Saxon fonts, or any so ancient, in
Cornwall or Wales, Guernsey or Anglesea. The
Saxon font, perhaps, was a mark of civilization
which had not reached these parts; be it so.
Our object is to shew that the Celtic custom was
to have the baptistery distinct from the church.
The earliest fonts in these places are of a late Norman date; and the strong similarity which exists
between them, in their peculiar shape and character, is a proof of the intimate communion which
must have existed between these places to a comparatively late period. Thus far have we traced
this custom; St. Piran's, let it be remembered,
has *no font*, but a spring " beside it."

Let us now turn to Ireland. With respect to
the baptistery, we find precisely the same custom
throughout Ireland, where it had been introduced from the East by the same people, the
Romans, in the time of Constantine, if not before. We read of St. Patrick baptizing a royal
convert near Dublin at a well, in the beginning
of the fifth century. We read of St. Kyeran's
well, near his monastery; St. Kyeran is none
other than our worthy tutelary St. Piran. Beside this well he lived and taught in his own
country before he came to Cornwall; and a great

many other instances may be cited. But let it
suffice to give but one more, which will shew
us that the custom continued so late as the tenth
century, and was followed by the Danes, who
conquered and settled among the Irish, and were
converted by them. In Grose's Antiquities of
Ireland there is an account of St. Dolough's
church, which was built by the Danes in the
tenth century. He says, "Beside it there is a
holy well of great celebrity;" "it is enclosed within an octagon building." Though the learned
antiquary does not tell what was the purpose of
this building, its shape and position near the
church at once decide the point. The octagon
is a baptismal figure; the No. 8, a baptismal
number.   St. Ambrose, in the fifth century,
writes of the octagon as symbolical of the new
and perfect Dispensation, of which holy Baptism
is the great initiatory rite. The No. 7 was symbolical of the natural Creation, which was per-
fected in seven days ; the No. 8 indicates another
degree of perfection beyond that, namely, which
was effected by our Lord's glorious Resurrection
on *the eighth day*. This mighty triumph over
death and the grave fully established the new
Dispensation under which we live, the perfect
and last Dispensation of trial, of which holy Baptism is a great and indispensable feature. Baptism is the gate of Christian life, and affords admission to all the blessed hopes and privileges of

that state purchased for us and sealed to us by the Resurrection on the eighth day ; hence the application of the perfect octagon to baptismal purposes : it has an intentional meaning, and was adopted at a very early period, and continues to this day the general and appropriate form of fonts. St. Ambrose, in the fourth century, writes thus of this symbolical figure :

> " Octachorum sanctos templum surrexit in usus,
> Octagonus fons est, munere dignus eo.
> Hoc numero decuit sacri baptismatis aulam
> Surgere, quo populis vera salus rediit.
> Luce resurgentes Christi, qui claustra resolvit
> Mortis, et a tumulis suscitet exanimes."

We have shewn, then, by our protracted assimilations, which however have been as brief as we could make them, that St. Piran's corresponds with the churches of the fourth century, and, as far as we have been able to trace, with those of the Celtic Christians of these islands ; we have endeavoured also to trace several important points of difference between this structure and those of the Saxons : let us now in conclusion turn our thoughts to Ireland. Here we shall find most interesting and striking similarities—all the peculiarities which St. Piran's possesses,—the distinct baptistery, the adjacent cell, the smallness of the edifice, the scarcity of windows, the round-headed doorway ornamented with *three heads*, and the raised threshold, the nave and chancel di-

vided, the stone altar and stone seats, and, lastly,
the rude masonry, constructed without *the use of
lime:* all these we find in Ireland, from whence
St. Piran came hither.

It is surprising what a great number of ruins
there are of this kind in that island : surprising,
we say, because they are so little known, and
theories of British early architecture or masonry have been formed without mention of this
very large class of authorities. It is true they
are not strictly British, but the intimate connection between Ireland and Britain in early
times is quite sufficient to justify allusion to
them as specimens of the early structures of this
island ; and more especially as we have remains
of churches, and records of many more, similar
in character to these. First, let us visit the spot
where St. Piran (in Ireland called Kyran) ministered previous to undertaking the charge St.
Patrick laid upon him in Cornwall. It is situated in King's County in Ireland, and called
at this day " Seir-Kyran," in honour of its tutelary Saint and former minister. In this neighbourhood, which was his native place, or, at any
rate, in his native province of Ossory, St. Kyran
first began his ministrations, after his return from
Rome. "Here he built a cell* beside a spring
in a place encompassed with woods," near a stream

* Probably derived from the Irish " ceall-cill-kil," a temple
or a church.

called "Fueran," and at St. Patrick's request
founded a monastery, or a house of regular canons
of *St. Austin*. His mother, whom he converted
and baptized, also presided over a monastery or
convent, to which a *church* was attached, called
" *Ceall* Lidair," in this neighbourhood. We are
informed by kind correspondents, that at *Seir*-
Kyran, in King's County in Ireland, there are to
this day ancient ruins situated a little westward
of a stream called *Fueran*, and that near the
ruins there is a well called " St. Kyran's Well."
The ruins of the walls which formed what we
suppose was the "Ceall" of St. Kyran, indicate
that it was " very small :" on the south-east corner
of it there is a round tower, evidently one of the
ancient ones of this country. The masonry of
the ruin and tower corresponds : it is very rude,
and formed of *uncut stone* put together *without
lime in the mortar*. In the east wall of the present parish church, which is in miserable repair,
is inserted the grotesque figure we here represent.
It is about sixteen or eighteen inches high, and
seven in breadth, and is executed in a " *soft white
stone*." This figure is called, and looked upon,
as an ancient " statue of St. Kyran," the patron
Saint of the place. In size and character, it will
be readily admitted, the " statue" is peculiar
enough ; but, strange to say, the head of this
figure corresponds exactly with two of the heads
which ornamented the doorway of St. Piran's, of

ANCIENT STATUE OF ST. KYRAN.

which we have given a representation above.
The projecting ears, the peculiar lines by which
the features of the face are delineated, correspond
exactly, line for line, with the heads alluded to,
which are in the Museum in Truro. Evidently
these were copied from the figure itself, or executed by the hand of the same ingenious sculptor
of remote times. The position in which the
figure is carved is singular, and may also have
its meaning, if we did but know it.

It will be observed the Saint is sitting in a
very unnatural posture, and shewing his heels ;
indeed it seems the great effort of the position
that he should shew his heels. The word "Seir,"
in the name "Seir-Kyran," signifies a "*heel ;*"
but what connection there is between these in-
cidents, or what interesting legend ought to be
known concerning the Saint's heels, we have not

been able *yet* to discover. The date of this figure
we suppose must be subsequent to the period of
the Saint's departure from the place of his first
ministration : probably it was executed as a monument to his memory soon after, and we should
add, very soon after, his departure ; for the history of the progress of the arts in Ireland would
lead us to expect better specimens of it even so
early as the sixth century. St. Kyran lived in
this place in the middle of the fifth : at this
time, and before this period, we may suppose
it was a place of importance, for there are many
remains of early military defences, such as fosses
and ramparts ; among them, in pretty good preservation, is a square encampment, formed by a
turf rampart and ditch. The ancient name of
this place was " Saiger," derived, it is supposed,
from " Saigeoir," a sawyer, " owing to the wooden
buildings* of which the town was originally composed." There can be little doubt that the stone

---

* About eight or nine years since, an ancient Irish wooden
house was discovered by some men who were probing a peat-
bog (with long iron rods). Captain Mudge, in a letter to the
Antiquarian Society, minutely describes this house : " It was
built of rough timber *rudely split*, and evidently belonged to a
period or a people *who knew not the use of iron*. Within the
house was found a wedge or chisel of stone, sharpened at one
end ; this instrument had been used for mortising the principal
timbers and posts of this house together. The house was only
twelve feet square, had a flat roof, and was in good preservation."

buildings now in ruins, together with the round tower, were in existence in the time of St. Kyran. We here beg to insert an extract from the Dublin Penny Journal,* on the subject of the latter, which is not only interesting, but valuable and conclusive on the point; but without further comment we will give it: " By far the most curious thing at Seir-Kyran's is the round tower, and to which I have never seen a similar one. It is only about twenty feet high, with a conical stone roof, and was evidently erected subsequent (?) to the fabric that once stood beside it, and against the south-east angle of which it is built. It contains a great many loopholes around it. These are three or four inches square on the outside, but are bevelled off so as to adjoin each other on the inside; some of the holes are not on a level with the others. I suppose this tower to have been used for keeping up a consecrated fire in it. These religious fires were by no means so rare

---

* This Journal, together with the Dublin Penny Magazine, which interesting publications are unfortunately given up, is one of those valuable works we have been able to find on the subject of Irish antiquities. We have reason to be assured that the statements in them are correct, and acknowledge to have drawn the greatest part of our Irish information from them. We believe we are indebted to the Journal for the representation, inserted above, of St. Kyran. We have also great pleasure in making our many acknowledgments to the ready and obliging correspondents we have had the honour to meet with in Ireland.

as some suppose. This is not a convenient place
for entering upon a dry and lengthened treatise
respecting them ; suffice it, therefore, to remark
that the Druids kept fires ignited as emblems
of the sun or life.

" In Toland's history we find, that on a certain
evening all the people of the country, out of a
religious persuasion instilled into them by the
Druids, extinguished their fires entirely ; that
every master of a family was obliged to take a
portion of the consecrated fire home, and to kindle
the fire anew in his house, which for the ensuing
year was to be lucky or prosperous. Macgeogha-
gan, tom. i. p. 81, writes : ' There was an annual
Druidical fire lighted at Ilachta, in the Barony
of Clonlisk, in King's County.' The same historian tells us, that this was an institution of the
monarch Tuathal-Teachmar, and that the place
it was held in had been cut off from Munster by
the same king. He adds, it was forbidden to
supply fires with fuel in November eve until they
were first renewed from that holy fire. We
are informed by early writers that this practice
was continued after the introduction of Christianity. We are *told that St. Patrick** had his

* This was probably at Downpatrick, *where there is a
round tower.* The monastery in this place, the ruins of which
adjoin the tower, was founded by the apostle of Ireland early
in the fifth century, on a hill (dûn) granted to him by the
chieftain of the Dal-dechu, who had been converted to Chris-

'consecrated fire;' and St. Brigid had, at Kildare, her 'perpetual fire.' Ware, in his 'Antiquities,' c. 17, § 6, informs us that Henry de Loundres, Archbishop of Dublin, ' put out St. Brigid's fire, because the custom was not used elsewhere.' It is strange how so learned a writer as Sir James Ware could have fallen into so great a mistake. In a paper by Mr. Cooke of Birr, giving an account of the Barnaari-Cuilawn, (a curious ancient ' fire-cover' in that gentleman's possession,) published in the Transactions of the Royal Irish Academy, as read before that learned body in the year 1822, he shews that relic to have been the cover of the perpetual fire instituted in the parish of Glankeem, County Tipperary, by St. Cuilawn, brother to Cormac M'Cullenan, who was King and Bishop of Cashel upwards of 900 years ago. In like manner St. Kyran had his consecrated fire at Saiger, in imitation of the Druidical

tianity by him. Here the body of St. Patrick was buried in the year 493. Cambrensis relates that his remains, together with those of SS. Brigid and Columba, were discovered by Sir John de Courcy in the year 1185, with the following epitaph over them:

Hi tres in Dûno tumulo tumulantur in uno,
Brigida, Patricius, atque Columba pius.

Sir John obtained a bull from Pope Pius Urban III. for the removal of these relics, and placed them in shrines within the abbey, which he greatly repaired and beautified. There is a round tower at Kildare also, near the monastery founded in the year 453 by St. Brigid, who was originally buried here, but subsequently removed to Downpatrick.

fire at Ilachta, which was but a short distance
from his monastery. Colgan (de Vita S^i Kierani,
c. 35, p. 462,) relates, ' *St. Kyran, the Bishop, resolved that the fire consecrated at Easter should not
be extinguished in his monastery for the whole
year.*' The same authority informs us that a
' boy named Chichideus, of Cluain, who belonged
to the monastery of Clonmacnoise, having spent
some days with St. Kyran at Saiger, extinguished
the fire, and was killed by wolves as a judgment
from heaven ; which when his master, St. Kyran
the younger, Abbot of Clonmacnoise,* learned,
he went to Saiger to St. Kyran, and was received

---

* Clonmacnoise, in King's County, is now one of the shrines
of some of the most valuable and interesting antiquarian
remains in Ireland. It is a poor village, but covered with
ecclesiastical ruins, and hallowed by so many undistinguished
graves of kings, nobles, and bishops, as to be aptly designated
the Iona of Ireland. The consecrated ground encloses about
two Irish acres, on which are the remains of the cathedral or
ancient abbey and *nine other small churches.* Here, also, *is a
round tower* at the north-east angle of one of the " small
chapels." The windows of the tower are pointed, but they
are clearly a later insertion. The tower itself, and the fabric
beside it, are very venerable in appearance, and claim a remote
antiquity: at the *west end* of the latter there is a small doorway with a rude round-headed *arch ornamented with three
heads, as was the doorway in our oratory;* one on the *key-
stone, and one on each side at the spring of the arch.* There is
one small window on the south side, and there may have been
one in the east wall. A monastery was founded here by St.
Kyran about the end of the fifth century.

K

with great honour, but there was *not then any fire in the monastery*, because the fires all through the place used daily to be *kindled from the consecrated fire*.'

" This story, divested of what relates to the wolves, plainly shews that there was formerly a sacred fire kept up here, and it is most likely the tower I have described was used as the fire-house. Such is at least my opinion, which I offer for the correction of those more learned in these matters." An opinion, moreover, which has some reasonable probability, as examination of the tower itself, and reference to a work by L. C. Beaufort, which obtained a prize offered by the Royal Irish Academy, will satisfactorily prove. It is clearly shewn in that work that these towers were originally introduced by Sun worshippers, and for the purpose alleged, of preserving in them the consecrated fire, the emblem of the Sun, and for which purpose they continued to be used in Christian times. But it is insisted by others that these structures are not to be assigned to the pagan times, but to the early Christian of Ireland; moreover, that they were not fire-houses, (which affects our argument materially,) but observatories or watch-towers, used also for the keeping of vestments and vessels of the church, and even as the dwellings of the attendant minister. It would be out of place here to enter minutely into this subject ; it is a subject on which much has been said, and several Irish prizes awarded. But, whatever their purpose really was, it seems more likely that they were receptacles of the sacred fire, than observatories, or watch-towers, or vestries, or hermitages! As observatories, to be good observatories and effectual, they would in reason have possessed more windows and loop-holes for the purpose of watching; and, as to their being vestries and hermitages, we cannot but imagine that they would have been more comfortable if erected in a more convenient shape for that purpose. The tower at Seir-Kyran, how-ever, has no loop-holes for watching, but has air-holes around it, such as we should look for in a fire-house; and it is not unlikely that the lower portion, the ground-floor, was the dwelling of the attendant on the fire and the church.

It is contended, in a paper in the 9th volume of Archæologia, that these towers were not fire-houses, but *bell-towers*, and therefore not pagan! In the East, near Jerusalem, there are several towers, not round, but square, in which bells were hung; and in one of them no less than three hermits lived in the different stories of the tower, one above the other! But this is by no means conclusive that these structures were always, from the beginning, assigned to such use, or that they were not anterior to Christian times. It would not injure the bell and hermit theory to believe that they were pagan edifices, and used for re-

ceptacles of consecrated fire ; and that, after
paganism had been dispelled and the fire extinguished, these towers were used as bell-
towers : and it is very probable indeed that
hermits should have climbed up into the deserted
towers — they loved such remote and secluded
places.   We can imagine a hermit looking out
of the loop-holes,—several of them in one tower,
looking out different ways from their respective
loop-holes, and fancying themselves all alone,
without at all overthrowing, nay, rather support-
ing, our theory that the places thus occupied had
once been used for a different purpose !   That
they were introduced into Ireland from the East
is probable, and indeed the fact ; and it adds much
interest to them on that account : Sun worship
and Druidism also, not only Christianity, were
introduced from the same quarter.   We refer our
readers to the note below for further proof that they
were used in early times as fire-houses, and even
in Ireland.*   Consecrated fire is a common ob-

* At Kinneigh, near the parish church, is a round tower
about seventy feet high.   It contains *only four small apertures
for air and light;* one facing west, another south-west, and
the others at opposite sides and different heights, all corresponding to the floors now gone. A stone-flagged floor
remains at the landing from the doorway, in the centre of
which is a square opening, large enough to admit a man to
go down into the dark chamber.   The neighbouring peasantry
are quite ignorant of the original use of this tower, they simply
call it " *cillcagh ;*" a name, however, sufficiently indicative of

ject of worship among the heathen in the East, who regard it as an " emblem of the Sun:" the

its meaning and also its heathen original. " Cill " signifies a temple or place of worship, and " agh " fire. (In Persia, and other places in the East, the same word is still used.) They state that it was erected by holy men in former times. The " cillcagh" announces at once a fane devoted to that form of religion compounded of Sabœism, or star-worship, and Budhism, of which the Sun was the principal deity in all the kindred mythologies of India, Persia, Phœnicia, Phrygia, Samothrace, and Ireland. Zerdust, or Zoroaster, the " Persian reformer," was the first who had Pyreia and fire-temples erected. Hanway tells us he saw four of them at *Sari :* they were composed of most durable material, round, about thirty feet in diameter, and one hundred and twenty feet high. Lord Valencia describes two round towers he saw in India, near Bhaugulpore, his lordship observes: " They resemble those buildings in Ireland." In the early annals of Ireland there is mention of " *Muighe Tuireth* na-bh-Fomoroch ;" that is, the Plain of the Fomorian Towers: " Maytura," the Tower in Mayo : " Turinnis," the Island of the Tower. The Tower of Temor, and many others, are mentioned with reference to a most remote period of Irish history. The Ulster Annals, in the year 448, record the occurrence of a terrible earthquake by which *fifty-seven towers* were destroyed and injured. The " Annals of the Four Masters," in the year 890, mention " the Turaghan Angcoire," the Fire-tower of the Anchorite at Inis Cailtre, an island in the Shannon. The same Annals, in the year 995, tell that Armagh was destroyed by lightning ; its hospital, cathedral, palace, and *Fidhnemead,* or " celestial index." These remarks shew their origin and purpose; that they were applied afterwards for Christian purposes is not improbable. It is even probable that they were so used, and also that others were built by the Christians. It is striking that so many of the remains of monasteries and churches founded by holy men and

shape of the tower pointing upward to the sky
seems appropriate to the purpose.

Why may not Christian missionaries have also
adopted this heathen custom with respect to fire
and tower also ? It is probable they did ; for
doubtless there were household superstitions connected with the sacred fire, and it was reasonable
and politic, in order to win souls, to follow the
same custom, though not necessarily with the pagan meaning : nay, it is due to policy and the earnest
character of the time to suppose that the Christian minister likewise had his sacred fire, for the
same reason that the Druids had theirs. It was
a significant custom to adopt, and one likely,
under the circumstances, to have been a very
effectual means of " winning souls," and moreover of keeping them, by bringing them continually to the minister of the true God, and to
His Church, for a fresh supply of the sacred fire.
It is a significant custom ! Did all Christians every-
where kindle the sacred fire of devotion *daily* at
the Temple of the Lord, the sincere and faithful
ministration of His servants would be more effectual, and the homes of their respective flocks
would not be dark or gloomy ; but the pleasant
cheerful light of peace would shine upon them,

women of the fifth and sixth centuries have generally a tower
near them ; generally speaking, they are on the north and east
angle of the church, with a communicating doorway : we shall
have occasion to refer to these hereafter.

and light them onward through the necessary
toils and trials of this world, even through bitter
trials, still cheerfully and thankfully to the end.
We have only one more short quotation, and then
we will go onward with our subject. We find
it was the general practice of the early clergy to
place their churches on the site of Druidical fanes,
and to seek to consecrate places which were already
endeared by the superstitions of a pagan people, to
the purposes of the true religion. " Thus in the
old life of St. Mocteus, by a writer of the seventh
century, it is related, that, when he came to Louth,
he found the place in possession of the *magi ;*
whereupon he lighted a fire, which they seeing
endeavoured to extinguish, lest their own idola-
trous fire should fail, but Mocteus proving victor
founded his monastery there :" and it is an interesting fact, *there is a round tower here also.*

But we have wandered long and far about
the use of round towers, but we trust not in vain,
or without an object. The quotations which we
have already made on the subject of the consecrated fire of St. Kyran will decide in some measure the date of the ruins at Seir-Kyran, and
thus render it not entirely incredible or impossible that a STONE *church* could have been erected
so early as the fifth century, or the beginning of
the sixth, in Cornwall ; and by St. Piran, who had
already built a church (ceall) and round tower
in Ireland. This removes the greatest difficulty,

with respect to the date we ask for the oratory of St. Piran; namely, that stone structures were not usual at this period. It is true, our examples are in Ireland: but St. Piran came from Ireland; and it is hoped that the precise similarity we are able to shew between St. Piran's and the ancient stone churches of Ireland will, if not prove, at least induce us to believe that they are contemporaneous.*

Ireland abounds with ruins,—ruins of magnificent churches and abbeys despoiled and torn down, and ruins also of a humbler class, which have no beauty, but much interest and their *rudeness* to recommend them; we refer to the ruins of old churches in Ireland, called "*Damhliags*," which are supposed to have been erected in the period immediately subsequent to the departure of the Romans, and prior to other foreign invasion. There are a very great number of these ruins throughout that country: they are no longer used for the sacred purposes of their erection; time and the destroyer have despoiled them, but they are not profaned. Veneration, or super-

* Here we should say, that, though driven by the scarcity of evidence to urge the probability that the model upon which this oratory is built is derived from Ireland, we are by no means disposed to make this the general rule in every case; for, after all we have said and quoted, we beg to maintain still that the art was derived from the Romans in both places, not in Cornwall from Ireland only: this, it will be observed, will also account for the alleged similarities.

stition be it called, still clings to them ; their hallowing influence is not scorned or despised. The sacred precincts of most of these churches are enclosed to this day, and used as " favourite burial-places." Almost every cemetery contains also *a spring*, and a hermitage or chamber for the dwelling of the attendant minister of the oratory. The churches lie east and west : the doorways are principally in the west or south ; and a small doorway in the north-east corner, which generally communicated with a round tower or cell.

At Clonmacnoise, where a " monastery" was founded by St. Kyran, there is a doorway which corresponds, as we have mentioned before, with St. Piran's ; it has a round archway, and is ornamented with three heads, one on the key-stone, and one on each side at the spring of the arch. Other peculiarities, such as the smallness of the church, the scarcity and diminutive size of the windows, we find also prevail in these structures. At the island of Inniscattery, near the mouth of the Shannon, in the fifth century St. Sennanus (who also built a church in Cornwall near the Land's End, where a parish is still dedicated to his memory,) erected eleven churches, whereof only seven now remain, but of these only three are supposed to be untouched. One called "Simon's Own," standing to the north-west of the cathedral, is not more than *twenty-three feet long*.

" Teampul-an-eird," that is, " the Temple on the
Height," is of similar dimensions and equally un-
adorned. The light is admitted into each of
these " Liliputian temples" by one or two very
small windows, little superior to loop-holes ; so
narrow, that, when entirely open, we must be
struck with surprise how the light which they
admitted could have sufficed. There is a round
tower among these ruins.

Again, there is the damhliag or little stone
church of St. Nissan, in an island called Ireland's
Eye, near Howth. This structure was built by
St. Nissan in the sixth century : at this place he
founded a monastery, to which he gave a copy of
the sacred Gospels. The ruin is 24*ft. by* 12*ft.* :
the walls are composed of *rough pebbles* and fragments of flint, which give an evidence of very remote antiquity. There are no traces of windows
but in the north, where there is an aperture which
may possibly have contained one, but that must
have been a mere loop-hole. There is a round tower
at the north-east angle of the ruin, and a small
chamber near it : this was probably the priest's
dwelling. At Trummery, in County Antrim,
there is a ruin of a church 40ft. by 15ft. : it *presents
nothing worthy of regard or notice with respect to
architecture.* The west gable, which has but one
pointed window, the only window of the church,
is entire ; but it was evidently a late insertion,
and speaks for the antiquity of the remainder of

the church. The door is on the south side. On
the north-east corner of the ruin is a round tower,
with a cell or apartment beside it, between it and
the church. One of the earliest of the old
churches in Ireland is that at Banagher in Lon-
donderry; it is supposed to have been built in
474. It is small: the door is *raised from the
ground;* it appears the steps to it were of stone.
The tradition is, that "O'Heney the Saint" was
the founder of the church, and that he used to
shew himself occasionally from this *raised threshold.* But let it suffice to look at one more place.
This is one of great interest, the valley of Glen-
dalough, where are ruins of seven churches.*

The first of these is now called the "Ivy
Church," is very small, and was, like all the "damhliags" of Ireland, roofed with flat stones. Not far
from this ruin is a small building, "probably the
sacristy, where reliques and vestments were kept."
The next is called the "kitchen" of St. Kevin,
who was the founder of these churches. It is the
most perfect of the seven, is roofed with stone, and
has a steeple resembling a *round tower,* but of mi-
niature proportions. It was lighted by only one
window. The interior measures twenty-two feet

---

* Besides the seven churches in this romantic valley, there
are seven at Clonmacnoise, seven at *Inniscalty,* " seven altars "
at Holy Cross, seven at Clonfert: " the same mystic number
may be traced throughout Ireland," probably adopted in allusion to the seven Churches of the East.

in length and sixteen in breadth ; at the east
end is an arch which communicates with a small
chapel. The chancel is 10ft. 6in. by 9ft. 3in., in
which there is a *small* east *window* or loop-hole.
In this chancel are the remains of a stone altar.
The remaining five correspond with these, and
have been described so often that it is needless
to trespass longer upon patience and indulgence
with " examples." There is a round tower among
these *ruins also*.

The similarity which we have traced between
St. Piran's and the early structures of the Irish
Christians not only cannot fail to strike us as such,
but there is another point of view which renders
the similarity of so much the more consequence to
our purpose ; namely, that, agreeing among themselves, these structures differ from those of the
Saxons and Normans. Whether these peculiarities,
which we find in St. Piran's, were introduced from
Ireland, or whether they were derived in Britain
and also in Ireland from the identical source, the
Romans, is not of so much importance as the
point that they—peculiar and agreeing in themselves—differ from Saxon structures, and more
still from Norman. If it be shewn that they do
not belong to either of these periods or people,
they necessarily belong to an earlier.

We have elsewhere, in the early part of the work,
remarked on the art of building with stone ; but,
with all deference to existing theories on the sub-

ject, it does not appear that it was wholly unknown in these islands prior to its practice by the Saxons. It would be assuming our argument to offer St. Piran's as an example of it : but there are amphitheatres and hill-castles in Cornwall built of stone ; and the structures in Ireland, under the circumstances we have already mentioned, may also be regarded as specimens of the art prior to any communication with the Saxons ; nay, it is yet to be proved that the latter did not learn the art from the Irish, among other arts of civilization introduced by that people. Assuming then that the art of building with stone in Cornwall was anterior to the time of the conquest of it by the Saxons in the tenth century, let us briefly examine the masonry of St. Piran's as compared with that of the Saxons and Normans.

First, the rudeness of the masonry. In this respect the oratory of St. Piran differs materially from well-authenticated Saxon buildings : there are no *hewn or cut stones,* no long and short arrangement in the quoins, no regular layers of " *work,*" no lime in the mortar, no string-courses or mouldings on the doorways or windows or in other parts of the church, except on one of the doorways, and that, we think, is not Saxon. The masonry of this structure we have already described : in rudeness it surpasses every Saxon structure we have ever seen, while, on the other hand, it resembles that of the Romans in the peculiar manner in which the stones are imbedded in the mortar; they do not appear to have been laid one by one upon each other in regular layers, but thrown together in some unaccountable way, some of the large stones resting upon the lower ones by their angles; but they have no layers of tiles or flat stones to bind the work according to the Roman manner. Again, there is no lime used in the masonry, but a white substance resembling it in appearance, though by no means in efficacy : it is evident from this that the use of lime, or of the manner of preparing it for use, was not known by the builders of this church; we cannot suppose it was omitted for the sake of economy. This is not the character of the time, they to whom we refer " did not sit down to count the cost of glorifying God ;" it must have been quite as expensive to have procured the China clay, which is used, as lime, for it is not to be had nearer than fourteen miles. Evidently, then, they knew not the use of lime.

Grose, in his " Antiquities of Ireland," informs us that the *Irish* did not know the use of lime till the ninth century, when the Danes taught it to them ; and if in Ireland the use of it was not known—Ireland was at this time the academy of the West—it is not to be wondered at that in Cornwall it was unknown also. If these remarks will apply to Saxon remains, they apply yet more to Norman, which are so much more perfect in material as also in construction. Again, the diminutive size of St. Piran's does not accord with Saxon and Norman structures, the scarcity of windows and their smallness. The Saxon and Norman churches had more windows and larger ones, and, besides that, had glass in them ; here there are no signs whatever of glass (it was introduced among the Saxons in the eighth century) : there are no grooves* for frames in the two windows *we boast of* in St. Piran's ; that in the east wall, indeed, was plastered throughout the splay, when discovered.

There is certainly an *internal splay* in the windows, though not in the doorways ; but this has not been shewn to be peculiarly Saxon or Norman. It seems probable, even from the reason of the case, that the same ingenuity which devised an aperture in a wall to admit air and light, would also devise to have as much of the latter as possible without the inconvenience of too much of the former : the internal splay seems naturally to have this twofold object. Besides the manner in which the head of the arch is formed, we should certainly say the art was derived from the masonry of the Romans ; it is formed, as reference

---

* The apparent groove in the south window represented in our ground-plan is only the intermediate space between the two layers of stone which form the window externally and on the inside ; the groove is very irregular, according to the sizes of the stones of which it is formed.

to our illustration will shew, with flat stones, resembling in shape Roman tiles, arranged side by
side, without any moulding or even chamfer on the
outer or inner angles. The doorways are round-
headed, without a splay, or chamfered angles ; and
that at the north-east corner, the priest's door,
without any moulding or other ornament. At
the principal entrance on the south side there is
a moulding, but it is not only unlike any Saxon
or Norman moulding we have ever met with, but
it differs from them by being carried up the sides
and round the head of the arch, without any capital or base ; and besides, there are three heads
arranged about it, at the key-stone, and on either
side of the doorway at the spring of the arch ;
which was not a Saxon or even a Norman feature, but one *which is found in Ireland in a
structure supposed to have been erected to St.
Piran*, at Clonmacnoise. If there is a peculiarity
in a Norman doorway more striking than another, it is the massive pier with capital and base
on each side, and the moulding of the arch resting on the capital ; in larger doorways a string of
mouldings is sometimes carried down the side of
the pier : but we know of no instance of a Norman
doorway without *capital or base ;* and the Saxon,
if anything, had more massive and conspicuous
capitals and bases to the doorways. We have
specimens of Norman masonry and architecture in
this county which are not inferior to those in other

counties ; which, placed beside the oratory of St. Piran, would at once indicate all we have been contending for. We have even evidence of Norman skill in this parish which is far above any that is displayed in the little structure in question. In No. vi. of the Illustrations of Baptismal Fonts there is a representation of the Norman font, which is still used and in good preservation, in this parish ; reference to this will shew that it is rather of an early Norman date, but still indicates a much later date than any portion of the oratory of St. Piran.

And lastly, to sum up our arguments and to bring them to a close, we have endeavoured to prove that this church corresponds with the models we have in the writings of the Fathers and historians of the fourth century ; that it corresponds, as far as we are able to ascertain, with the structures erected by the British about the same time in this country ; that, differing from Saxon and Norman structures, it corresponds exactly with those erected by the Irish both in Ireland and in Britain.

In short, we know what this church is like, and what it is not like ; that it resembles the earliest churches, and differs from Saxon and Norman : we may conclude, therefore, that it is British. The history of this parish, and a few other circumstances, will confirm the opinion. Our earliest record informs us that St. Kyran built a cell

L

beside a spring. It has hitherto escaped us that
the word translated " cell " in this instance means
" church," derived from the Irish " ceall" or " cill "
" kil," church ; the same term is used for the structure he erected in Saiger, or Seir-Kyran. The
next record informs us the name of this place
is *Lanpiran :* the word " Lan " is the British word
which answers to the Irish " Ceall," and, like it,
means church—the British church of St. Piran.
So early as the time of Edward the Confessor,
who was the son of Athelstan who conquered
Cornwall, and who made the first Register of
Cornish churches or ecclesiastical establishments,—
at this time there was a house of canons regular
here ; it will be remembered St. Kyran founded
similar establishments in Ireland, at Seir-Kyran
and Clonmacnoise.*

We need follow this history no further. It remains now to be judged whether this oratory was
erected by St. Piran himself, or soon after his

---

* We have just been favoured with another evidence of the
British antiquity of St. Piran's, by the sight of a ring and
portion of a brooch discovered on a skeleton which was buried
almost on a level with the foundation of the church, and therefore probably before its submersion. The ring, which is now
the property of Mr. Thomas Hoblyn, the representative of an
ancient family of this parish, is of silver, very massive, and has
an elongated zigzag pattern upon it, which corresponds exactly
with that which is found on British *sepulchral* urns ; and on
one side there is an attempt to represent the head of some
monster, serpent or dragon. We hope, through the medium of

departure, or whether it is Norman ; and this we
must leave to our candid readers to decide for
themselves.

We can only add, in conclusion, that there is
a strong probability that this oratory was overwhelmed before the conquest of Cornwall, under
Athelstan, by the Saxons, in the year 936 ; for
it is impossible to suppose that this little structure, with the humble dwelling beside it, formed
the collegiate establishment of Lanpiran, which
the Saxons found here, and which is mentioned in
the Register of Edward the Confessor. We are
inclined to believe that at this period the "monastery" stood on the opposite side of the stream
that proved so effectual a barrier from the sand,
and was located on that site which is now occupied by the ruins of the " second church."
The solitary granite cross which at present stands,
the sole monument of former days, among ruinous
heaps, is not a slight confirmation of this opinion ; for it is a Greek cross, and its venerable
and time-worn appearance also attests that it be-
longs to a period anterior to the introduction of

some antiquarian publication, to furnish the public with an
engraving of this interesting ring. The portion of the brooch
discovered is of copper. It was probably the pin of the
brooch ; it is twisted in the manner of the British torc or
collar, and is about two inches long; the remainder of the
brooch may have been composed of ivory or other material
which is now decomposed.

the customs of the Western or Latin Church into this country by the Saxons.

Lastly, it may be that we have arrived at conclusions not clear to others, and that we have put forward theories which cannot be supported ; but we trust we are open to conviction, and capable of conceding readily points which we have assumed inconclusively. The opinion we entertain of the oratory of St. Piran is, that it was built by St. Piran himself in the fifth century, or soon after by his successors; that it continued to be used for the holy purpose for which it had been erected for the space of two or three or perhaps four centuries, certainly not longer, if we may judge from the state in which it was found,—indeed, we can scarcely believe that it could have stood so long as four centuries previous to its submersion, rudely built as it is, and in a situation so exposed to violent storms ; that it was overwhelmed in the eighth or ninth century, and that another church was erected on the opposite side of the stream, in the cemetery of which church the " four-holed" Greek cross we have described was set up ; and to the religious establishment of this church we suppose the Register of Edward the Confessor to refer, under the name of " Lanpiran." After the Norman conquest the church was probably rebuilt, and a Norman font introduced into it, the same which still remains in use in this parish. In the year 1430 the church was again rebuilt, in the perpendicular style: such it remained till 1803, when it was deemed expedient to take it down and rebuild it elsewhere, which was accordingly done in the year following. The tower, porch, the pillars and arches, and windows, having been removed to a part of the parish called Lamborne, were again set up, and form a pretty country church, very creditable to those who built it, considering the low ebb of taste in church architecture at the time. Such is the history of the churches of St. Piran in Zabuloe.

There are records of another small church about one mile eastward of "the oratory :" a field near " St. Perran's Well," in a village called " Perran Well," is known by the name of the " Old Church," and within the memory of some of the inhabitants of the neighbourhood portions of " rude masonry" have been torn up at different times in ploughing the field and preparing it for the reception of seed. But this structure cannot be identified as the resting-place of St. Piran. It may have been built in his time, or soon after, or at any rate in British times; as also a small church which gave the village of Lamborne its name, Lan-bron, " a church on an enclosed hill;" and another at Callestoc Veor, " the great valley of oaks."

Lyson, in his History of Cornwall, informs us there were seven chapels in this Parish, and there are traces and traditions of as many still remaining.

If there be any portion of the evidence we
have adduced in support of the antiquity of St.
Piran's oratory which we would revert to, or
would urge before every other, in confirmation
of the British antiquity of this structure, it is
the internal evidence of antiquity which the masonry affords. It is, in fact, the great evidence;
all others are as a confirmation of it. It is a
portion of evidence, too, which is worthy of regard, not only on its own account, but also in
honour and respect to the memory of those who
reared this little edifice. Rudeness in a structure may proceed, it is true, from negligence or
ignorance, or from motives of pecuniary consideration ; but neither of these can be detected here.
Look at it as attentively as we will, there is rudeness, but also some care and a little thought too ;
there is unskilfulness, but also an effort to do the
best in the builder's power : these mark it at once
as the work of a people who did their best, and
therefore deserve our respect.   It would have
proved far more difficult to a Norman mason to
have arranged the stones in the way they are here
thrown together than to have laid them in regular
courses.

Again, the specimen of the carving in the
door-way, even on soft stone, confirms that they
had but imperfect instruments for their work.
Nothing can be ruder than the building itself,
and the three heads ; still they were put up, and

we cannot but believe put up as the best their simple art could produce to decorate their house of prayer. The interior of the church bears evidence of even still greater care and attention. It was smoothly plastered with china clay, which is perfectly white and clean, even after it has been buried in sand for centuries. All these taken together bespeak an effort which we must respect, though we cannot admire the result. As to the other motives mentioned, it is unnecessary to dwell upon them, for it is especially due to the character and piety of the time we treat of to exonerate them from such motives. It was their praise, as it has been well expressed, " that they did not sit down to count the cost of glorifying God." They gave freely of the best and costliest in their power ; it was their pride and happiness to be permitted to devote of their substance to the Lord. We regard the masonry of the church, therefore, as a strong evidence of its antiquity ; and, rude and imperfect as it is, still we look upon it with interest as the best and most perfect our primitive and simple brethren of early times were capable of devoting to the service and glory of our God.

THE END.

LONDON :
Printed by S. & J. BENTLEY, WILSON, and FLEY,
Bangor House, Shoe Lane.